# Interior Landscapes

RONALD REES

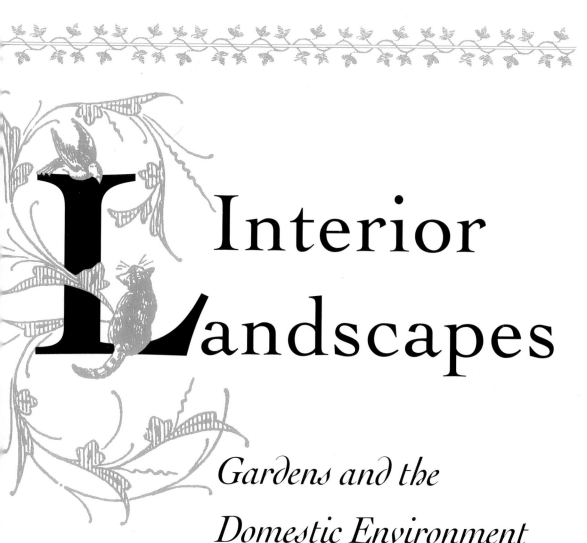

# Interior Landscapes

*Gardens and the Domestic Environment*

THE JOHNS HOPKINS UNIVERSITY PRESS / BALTIMORE AND LONDON

*To my favorite needlewomen:*
*Elizabeth Rees, my mother, and Mildred Collins,*
*my mother-in-law*


Published in cooperation with
the Center for American Places,
Harrisonburg, Virginia

© 1993 The Johns Hopkins University Press
All rights reserved
Printed in the United States of America
on acid-free paper

The Johns Hopkins University Press
2715 North Charles Street
Baltimore, Maryland 21218-4319
The Johns Hopkins Press Ltd., London

Photos by Stanley A. Jashemski are reprinted, by
permission of the author, from Wilhelmina F.
Jashemski, *The Gardens of Pompeii, Herculaneum, and
the Villas Destroyed by Vesuvius* (New Rochelle, N.Y.:
Caratzas Brothers, 1979).

Library of Congress Cataloging-in-Publication Data

Rees, Ronald, 1935–
Interior landscapes : gardens and the domestic
environment / by Ronald Rees.—1st ed.
p.    cm.
Includes bibliographical references and index.
ISBN 0-8018-4467-3
1. Interior decoration.   2. Nature (Aesthetics)
3. Mural painting and decoration.   4. Wallpaper.
5. Tapestry.   I. Title.
NK2113.R44   1993
747—dc20   92-536

# The garden's full of furniture and the house is full of plants.

Michael Flanders and Donald Swann,
"Design for Living," *At the Drop of a Hat*

# Contents

Acknowledgments ix

Introduction xi

PALACE AND VILLA 1

CLOISTER AND CASTLE 15

RENAISSANCE HOUSE AND GARDEN 37

OUTLANDISH LANDSCAPES 67

THE NEOCLASSICAL LANDSCAPE 93

NINETEENTH-CENTURY VILLAS 117

GARDENS INDOORS 147

EPILOGUE 167

Bibliography 179     Index 183

# Acknowledgments

Few books that are not wholly works of the imagination can be written without help from many sources, and this one was no exception. My heaviest debt is to the Social Sciences and Humanities Research Council of Canada for a travel grant that enabled me to visit libraries in Canada, the United States, and the United Kingdom. I owe, too, a large debt of gratitude to George F. Thompson, president of the Center for American Places and publishing consultant to the Johns Hopkins University Press, whose enthusiasm for the book never wavered, even during the most trying phases of its gestation. Also steadfast was his assistant, Margaret Gillespie, who came to my rescue when I had difficulty finding suitable illustrations for the final chapters. For the seamless stitching of rents in the text, I am indebted to Grace Buonocore, a skilled and gentle copy editor.

My debts to libraries and librarians are too numerous to detail, but two librarians must be singled out: Karen Herrick and Marilyn Diffin of the Calais Free Library in Washington County, Maine. Through them and the wonderfully efficient "MAINECAT" system, I was at the receiving end of a stream of books from both public and college libraries in Maine and New England. Communities along the mouth of the St Croix River, the political divide between Maine and New Brunswick, have always considered that the ties that bind them transcend national interests. Of that happy circumstance I am a fortunate and grateful beneficiary.

# Introduction

The room in which I work has, like most modern rooms, plain walls and a sizeable window. Color, shapes, and figures are confined to the curtains that frame the window and the carpet that covers the floor. The curtains show farmyard and hunting scenes copied from Elizabethan embroideries; the carpet has a dense pattern of leaves and flowers whose provenance is even older. This combination of plain walls and large windows with occasional nature- or landscape-inspired motifs on curtains, carpets, and upholstery may be found in countless houses across the North American continent. In the current decorative climate, landscape and naturalistic motifs are vestigial, but at times when they dominated both walls and furnishings, they altered the look and feel of entire rooms. Roman walls, for example, were covered with paintings of gardens and orchards, medieval and Renaissance walls with tapestries of the hunt and the pleasance, and nineteenth-century American walls with paper imprinted with vistas of Paris or Pompeii.

People in civilized societies, as the art historian Kenneth Clark reminded us, have always taken pleasure in a view, and in part this explains the persistence and popularity of gardens and landscapes as decorative motifs. But in the decoration of rooms there was another, and I think more powerful, impulse at work. Much room decoration was intended to create an *environment*, not simply to gratify the eye. For much of our history the surroundings most often appreciated for their comfort, color, and warmth were the garden and the spring and summer landscapes. Early houses were cold, damp, poorly lit, and malodorous, and they remained so until fuel, glass, fabrics, and paint became plentiful and heating, lighting, and drainage systems effective. They also lacked soft, comfortable seating. Outside, weather permitting, was always preferred to inside. Even Hadrian's famed villa at Prima Porta, the touchstone for luxury and comfort throughout much of European history, was probably not as comfortable as an average house in an average middle-class American suburb. In Roman Italy, where standards of housing were far above historical norms, life was lived out of doors as much as possible.

North of the Mediterranean, climate was less benign; housing, even for the rich, fell far below Roman standards until modern times. Winter was a dreaded season of cold days and long, dark nights, not the mere irritant it is today. "No enemy," Shakespeare could write, "but winter and rough weather." Winter nights could be cold enough to freeze the wine and damp enough to mildew the wall hangings. Spring and summer, by contrast, were glorious: Light, warmth, color, and fragrance dispelled "old December's bareness." They were relished with an intensity we now find difficult to appreciate. For most of us the summer landscape is a playground in which we barbecue, golf, sunbathe, and admire scenery; for our forebears it was a cornucopia of sensory delights and symbolic meanings. Gardens then were vital appendages accorded the kind of attention we now lavish on our interiors.

Since classical times one of the main objectives of house design and decoration has been to merge living space with the garden and the wider landscape. Large, removeable windows brought the garden indoors, and porches, pergolas, and garden and tree houses carried living space into the garden. Where there was no access to the garden, or no view, the outside was introduced symbolically; semblances and reminders of the garden and the summer landscape were created on walls, floors, and furnishings. Efforts at simulation ranged from simple to complex—from strewing floors and mantels with flowers, herbs, and branches to representing gardens and entire countrysides in wall paintings, tapestries, and embroideries. At first, interest in landscape focused on the garden and the landscape of the chase or the hunt, but as countrysides became safer, and nature more controlled, interest quickened in the world beyond the garden and the hunting park. Until the Renaissance the motifs were European, but reports from travelers to distant lands and the appearance in Europe of exotic artifacts and plants excited interest in the life and landscapes of the Near East, India, and China. Rugs from the Levant evoked the flavor of Persian gardens and hunting parks, and wallpapers from China offered the first glimpses of lives and landscapes that for centuries had tantalized Europeans.

The objective of this book, then, is to show how persistent *landscape* has been as a motif in decorative art and to explain the significance of this. The book is an exercise in the history of culture and environment, not in the history of art or design, and thus the emphasis is on the cultural significance of gardens, landscapes, and their constituent plants, not on the manner of their representation. And although coverings for floors and furniture receive appropriate attention in the book, my chief concern is the decoration of walls. I have taken to heart William Morris's axiom that the "feeling" of a room is determined chiefly by the treatment of the walls: "Whatever you have in your rooms, think first of the walls, for they are that which makes your house and home." In wall decoration, the focus is on pictures or pictorial effects, rather than pattern or design, and the lens through which they are examined has cultural sensors only. Representations of garden and countryside, whether painted, woven, or sewn, are regarded as expressions of landscape preference or taste, not as subjects of art.

This, then, is not a book about aesthetics. Easel paintings have been excluded from it, even though by conforming to the fashion of the period, they, too, were often an integral part of interior decoration. The modern distinction between fine and decorative art rests, in part, on a tendency to exaggerate the historical role of painting. Not until the Renaissance did it become the preeminent art, and for long afterward paintings were frequently ordered by patrons for particular places—to fit a wall panel or to fill an empty place over a door or a chimney piece. In such cases, size and subject were usually stipulated, and often treatment as well. George Washington, in 1757, ordered "A Neat Landskip 3 feet by 21 inches" for his mantelpiece.

In essence, *Interior Landscapes* is an extended essay based on a wide-ranging survey of the evolution of landscape and decorative art in the Mediterranean, continental Europe, and especially Britain and North America. As a motif in decorative art, landscape has persisted to the present, but with diminished vitality. Abstract tendencies in art have discouraged naturalistic representation of landscape. Nature, too, has lost much of its symbolic and emblematic meaning. And because we can now create interiors that are warm and well lighted, we no longer feel compelled to bring the outside inside.

# Interior Landscapes

# Palace and Villa

oan Evans, the renowned medievalist, once remarked that there are two prerequisites for naturalistic decoration: distance from wild nature, and buildings. Decoration needs a frame, and except for images scratched on weapons or vessels of bone, stone, and clay, one can speak of it only when space has been architecturally defined and nature, to some extent, organized and controlled. Though beautiful, the Paleolithic cave paintings are not decorative; the caves are dark and almost inaccessible, and the paintings are not composed. The animals were painted singly, and any juxtapositions seem to have been determined by the configuration of the walls of the caves, not the design of the artists.

Decorative art is chiefly a product of cities or of urbanized societies. In Europe it began in Crete. By the beginning of the second millennium before Christ, the cities of Minoan Crete were large enough to set people apart from wild nature, and, protected by the sea and a powerful fleet, they were secure enough for the practice of decorative art. No fortress walls restricted views of the countryside, and by framing those views, the openings of doors and windows and the angular lines of streets and porticoes enhanced them. At the same time, walls of alabaster in the courts and palaces presented settings and spaces well enough defined to invite decoration.

The dominant art form was fresco painting. Pigments mixed with water, or water and lime, were painted quickly onto wet lime plaster, and as the lime set, the pigments were bound to the plaster. Walls, ceilings, and even the floors of palaces and houses were decorated with frescoes. No complete paintings have survived, but the fragments show birds and other animals, leaves, fern sprays, spikelets of flowering rushes, and fields of crocuses. One of the largest pieces, which once adorned the walls of the royal palace in Knossos, shows a slim youth plucking yellow and white crocuses and arranging them in banks on the ground. The open, pillared halls and terraces of the palace at Knossos look down on a green, secluded valley that may once have held pleasure gardens.

Minoan eyes saw beauty in the sea as well as the land. Crete is bounded by a rocky and—to us, now—attractive coast, and it looked to the sea for its defense, its commerce, and its sustenance. Cretans fished the waters of the Mediterranean, dove in them for sponges, and dispatched upon them precious cargoes of oil, wine, and wool. The sea was an asset and an ally, and as if to acknowledge this, Cretan artists painted sponges, octopi, coral, cuttlefish, and underground reefs covered with seaweed. Painted fish decorated the floor of a shrine at Hagia Triada, and high on a wall in the queen's chamber in Knossos there was a frieze of leaping dolphins.

Greece, a country of cities, might have been expected to carry on the practice of naturalistic decoration, but the Greeks, unlike their island neighbors, had little interest in landscape. No Greek wall paintings have survived, but if painting in Greece followed the pattern of literature, then little of it would have reflected direct observation of nature. In the *Iliad*, for example, Homer concentrated on human action and event; there is land—the bloody littoral of Troy—but no caring and discerning eye to transform it into landscape. When nature is described, the approach is usually tangential, through the literary form of the simile. Yet in the *Odyssey*, where description of nature is more direct, Homer presented literature with its first ideal landscape. In the garden of Alcinoüs, the fruit trees bore year-round and the gentle Westwind always blew. But though blessed by the elements, and possessed of beauty and charm, Alcinoüs's garden was wholly functional; it had fruit trees and vegetables arranged in "fair ordered beds," but no one had yet hit upon the idea of transferring to the garden plot "the lovely children of the meadow." The Greeks were not floriculturists, and flowers hardly signified in their aesthetic. They were not brought indoors, nor were they used as motifs in the decoration of interiors or, for that matter, clothes. The open courts of palaces and larger houses, which were so important in the later development of gardening, were for the most part empty of plants. Most were paved, and only in the women's quarters would courts have had trees, shrubs in terra-cotta containers, and a few statues. Lucian said of a house of Aphrodite that it was not paved "in the usual way" but adorned, as was suitable to the lady of the house, with noble, shady trees, flowers, and arbors.

**ROMAN GARDENS**

Not until Roman times were there consistent expressions of feeling for landscape. Lucretius, Virgil, Horace, and Varro wrote a century before Christ about a countryside that they both loved and understood. An interest in things rural, *res rustica*, was a distinguishing mark of a Roman gentleman. Virgil's *Georgics*, a poem of the land, is as essentially Italian as the *Odyssey*, a poem of the sea, is essentially Greek. In the four books of the *Georgics* (37–30 B.C.), Virgil, whose father was a Lombard farmer, dealt systematically with all aspects of rural economy: "wheat and woodland / tilth and vineyard, hive and horse and herd." Romans in general were intensely conscious of the countryside, and not until Renaissance Italy or Georgian England would there be again the same conviction of the importance to the well-governed state of well-ordered land.

But as well as admiring fat soils and fine crops, the Romans loved gardens. The *hortus*, or garden plot, was an important part of the primitive *heredium* (family farm), and by adding flowers, flowering trees and shrubs, statuary, and fountains, the Romans made an ornament of it, a *viridarium*. By the first century B.C., many of the larger farms and estates had become leisure retreats (*villae urbanae* as distinct from *villae rusticae*), with large houses and ornamental gardens. In his *Natural History*, written during the middle of the first century A.D., the elder Pliny remarked that Romans were inclined to regard almost any piece of inherited land as a "garden," even though it was more properly a farm or an estate. Ornamental courtyard gardens were also an integral part of Roman town houses, and they could be found in temples, baths, theaters, schools, restaurants, and shops. Martial, in the first century A.D., poked fun at a man whose garden was so full of plants, walks, fountains, and statues that his household lacked space for eating and sleeping.

Except for their plebeian quarters, Roman towns must have looked like garden cities. Roof gardens, which were built on special substructures to protect the underlying roofs from damp, could be found in all but the poorest districts. Colonnade roofs were used in the same way. The owners of even small houses made gardens in tiny light wells or in small yards at the back of their properties. Apartment dwellers grew plants in window boxes; shop-keepers, confined to rooms above their shops, had to make do with a few vines grown on their balconies. Vines made a shady arbor. Shopkeepers who happened to live in quarters overlooking gardens sometimes cut openings in the walls so that they might enjoy the view. The gardenless could also buy flowers. Nurseries in Campania grew flowers especially for sale in the towns, and in Rome artificially heated forcing houses, fitted with translucent mica windows, produced winter-blooming roses and lilies.

Urban Romans who could afford to indulge their tastes made the garden the heart and center of their worlds. The larger houses looked inward to gardens and courtyards, turning their backs to the street. For privacy, windows on street walls were small and high, and sometimes they were glazed with filmy glass. An atrium, or partially covered central courtyard, was a standard feature of the larger, patrician houses, and the very largest houses had a second open area, or *peristyle*, around which rooms might also be arranged. In its original Greek, or Hellenistic, form, the peristyle was a courtyard paved with cobblestones, mosaic, or hammered earth, but in Roman hands the peristyle became a garden filled with plantings, pools, fountains, and sculptures. In late republican Rome, the atrium also became a garden. From the outset plants had been grown in boxes around the walls, but, with improvements in water supply and drainage, the centrally placed *impluvium*, a catch basin for rainwater and once a necessary adjunct to the house, became obsolete. The basin and cistern were converted into an ornamental pool connected by lead pipes or terra-cotta tubes to the city drains, and the space formerly reserved for the impluvium was taken up by fountains, shrubbery, and plants. Gardens were so valued that in dry Campania they were fed with precious aqueduct water.

In southern Italy, where life could be lived out of doors for much of the year, gardens were magnets. On summer afternoons and evenings, gardens and porticoes would have been far more enticing than hot, stuffy rooms, and Romans repaired to them as frequently as possible. Much of the work of the household was performed in the garden. Women spun and wove in the garden itself or in the shaded porticoes around it. Loom weights were found in all the gardens excavated at Pompeii. When the younger Pliny stayed at his Tuscan villa, it was his habit to think through his work and then dictate it either in his garden or in the covered arcade that adjoined it.

The garden was also a place for leisure and play. In summer most meals would have been taken out of doors or within sight and sound of the garden. Dining rooms (*triclinia*) usually looked onto gardens, and if these had pools or fountains, the diners would have eaten to the relaxing sound of splashing

A terrace that linked house and garden in the house of Loreius Tibertinus, Pompeii. Vines trained across the roof of the terrace provided shade in summer. At the far end of the terrace is an open-air dining room. (Stanley A. Jashemski)

water. "How inviting is your house, O Albucius," wrote one appreciative guest on a garden wall at Pompeii. For outdoor dining there were masonry dining couches made comfortable with mattresses and pillows and shaded with a vine-covered arbor or perhaps a curtain or *velum*. Sometimes the dining couches were surrounded by fish pools. "People," as Varro remarked, "used to eat in winter by the hearth, in summer out of doors."

One of the most elaborate outdoor dining areas was in Pliny's villa at Tifernum in Tuscany. It consisted of an alcove of white marble supported by four pillars and shaded by vines. From a bench in the alcove, water gushed through several small pipes into a cistern that fed a polished marble basin so artfully contrived that it never overflowed. When Pliny dined in the alcove, the basin served as a table; the larger dishes were placed around the edges, and the smaller ones, shaped as little boats or waterfowl, floated about on the water. Had Pliny wanted to rest after eating, there was, just beyond the dining area, a garden bedroom furnished with a couch. Though it had windows on every side, it enjoyed "a very agreeable gloominess," thanks to a spreading vine that entirely shaded it. "Here you may recline," Pliny remarked, "and fancy yourself in a wood, with this difference only, you are not exposed to the weather."

For Romans, the ideal habitat was one in which house, garden, and larger landscape were connected. Wherever possible, they achieved this architecturally. Town houses were built around gardens and courtyards, and the rooms opened onto them. Particular rooms, named "Cyzicene" after the city of Cyzicus in Persia, opened to the garden by means of windows that sometimes occupied the entire wall. The Persian models had a large horizontal panel across the top and vertical side panels that opened like doors. In other arrangements, the windows could be pushed upward or entirely removed so that in favorable weather the room became part of the garden.

While town houses looked inward to courtyards and gardens, country houses looked onto the Roman countryside. Those around Pompeii enjoyed views of the lovely Campanian plain: "the most blest of all plains," according to the Greek geographer Strabo, who lived in the first century B.C. The gardens of the villas were vestibules to the surrounding landscape. At Pliny's Tuscan villa, box hedging, cut in the form of steps, concealed the outside walls of the garden so effectively that the garden and the surrounding countryside appeared to be joined: "It is always an object of desire," Pliny noted, "that the front of the villa shall have a view over the landscape, where nature seems as good as the garden made by art." To unite nature and art, Hadrian deepened and roughened the Vale of Tempe, which adjoined the formal gardens of his villa at Tivoli, so that there would be a natural-seeming bridge between the gardens and the wild, wooded landscape of the Tiburtine hills.

# Palace and Villa

At Tivoli there was no "pale"; gardens, fields, valleys, and distant hills all merged to form a single, unified landscape.

**ROMAN WALL**

**PAINTINGS**

The Romans' need to feel connected with their surroundings determined the nature of indoor decoration. Where rooms did not open directly onto gardens, or did not command a view, Romans resorted to illusion; views of gardens and landscapes were painted onto interior walls or woven or sewn onto curtains, cushions, carpets, and wall hangings. Draperies and woven and embroidered wall hangings were part of the everyday furnishings of atrium-style houses. Only fragments of these soft furnishings have survived, but the historian Sallust once described the effect they had on visitors to city houses (the translation is Philemon Holland's, from the seventeenth century): "That a man could not heretofore come by a commoner's house within the citie, but he should see the windows beautified with green quishins [cushions], wrought and tapissed with flowers of all colors; resembling daily to their view the Gardens indeed which were in the out-villages, as being the very heart of the citie, they might think themselves in the countrey."

The interior walls of most houses in Pompeii and Herculaneum were covered with paintings. Rooms even in the larger houses tended to be narrow, small, poorly lit, and stuffy; few had windows that were more than mere slits in the wall, and many, in fact, were lighted and ventilated only by their doorways. Without embellishment and some form of artificial or illusionistic enlargement, many of them would have seemed like prison cells. The methods employed by Pompeian wall painters have been hotly debated, but it is generally agreed that the objective was to create reflecting surfaces. In a dimly lit room even a moderately reflecting surface can seem relatively bright. To increase reflectivity, the paint was applied to a topcoat of ultrafine plaster made from lime and marble dust. Both lime and marble were pulverized, and the fine mortar they made was "polished" by repeated troweling of the surface of the wall. Vitruvius's writings seem to indicate that the paint was then applied to the wet plaster in true fresco fashion, but subsequent investigators have suggested that Vitruvius may have been referring to the ground coloring only, not to the final painting. Finishing pigments were applied to the wet or dry surface with either a spatula or a fine brush, and to give them luster, they were mixed with heated wax. A final coat of polished wax on the surface of the painting added to its brilliance and also gave some protection.

One of the best-known attempts to create indoors an illusion of the outdoors is the wall painting in a large underground room in the villa of the

Wall painting in a large underground room of the villa of Livia, at Prima Porta. In a cool space 3 meters below floor level, the empress could enjoy the illusion of a garden. The painting, interrupted only by the doorway, covered all four walls. (Museo Nazionale, Rome)

Empress Livia at Prima Porta. The empress's declared aim was to create a cool space, 3 meters below the main-floor level, where she could enjoy a facsimile of her garden. On all four walls of the room—which was probably lighted from above—the scene is of a garden of massed flower beds, bordered by shrubs and fruit trees, retreating toward a gentle woodland. The beds lie behind a low latticed fence and are drawn with minute accuracy. Recesses in the walls harbor painted oaks and evergreen trees. Most frescoes were painted quickly and not always delicately by journeyman painters who did only as much as they were paid to do, but those at the villa of Livia are fine enough to have charmed Bernard Berenson, the art historian and connoisseur. After his visit, he noted in his diary: "How dewy, how penetratingly fresh the grass and trees and flowers, how coruscating the fruit."

Paintings of gardens also adorned the walls of baths, restaurants, and schools. Restaurants in garden settings were so popular in Pompeii that at least one owner had garden scenes painted on the walls of a small room so that in poor weather his customers might have the illusion of dining out of doors. Similarly, bathers in the confined rooms of city baths were able to feign the pleasures of bathing in the Campanian sunshine. Paintings on the walls of the *frigidaria* (cooling room) in both the Forum and the Stabian baths in Pompeii suggested that the pools were set in attractive gardens and countrysides. A garden painting was also found in a small building, identified as a school, where Pompeian youths received instruction in the teachings of Epicurus. On the walls of the front room, painted plants flower behind a lattice fence. To give the vestibule the appearance of a small garden, so investigators believe, potted plants were placed in front of the painted ones.

So appealing were garden paintings that they were popular even on the walls of tombs. In the street of tombs at Pompeii, the walls surrounding a monument that looks like a triclinium for outdoor dining were painted with plants and animals. Though flowers have long been symbols of regeneration, and Roman bodies were adorned with them at death, the tomb paintings and tomb gardens seem to have been more decorative than symbolic. At Pompeii, Trimalchio left the following instructions for his burial: "I should like to have all kinds of fruit growing round my ashes, and plenty of vines." A similar directive at Cirta tells how a Roman in Africa planned his tomb: "On my tumulus bees shall sip the thyme blossoms, the birds shall sing pleasantly to me in verdant grottoes; there buds the laurel, and golden bunches of grapes hang on the vines."

As well as reminding Romans of their gardens, wall paintings in houses and public buildings offered glimpses of wider landscapes. To open up the rooms, pillars or pilasters were painted on whose entablatures the real ceiling seemed to rest. Painters were then free to remove the walls and paint landscapes or prospects that, in an ideal world, might have lain beyond them. The elder Pliny attributed the fashion for painting prospects to a painter named Spurius Studius or Spurius Tadius. In the reign of Augustus, wrote Pliny, "[he] first introduced the most attractive fashion of painting walls with pictures of villas and porticoes and landscape gardens, sacred groves, woods, hills, fish-ponds, canals, rivers, coasts, and whatever anybody could desire, together with various sketches of people going for a stroll or sailing in a boat or on land going to country houses, riding on asses or in carriages, and also people fishing or fowling or hunting or even gathering the vintage." According to Pliny, he also used pictures of seaside cities to decorate the walls of uncovered terraces; these gave, noted Pliny, "a most pleasing effect . . . at a very small expense."

Vitruvius wrote in a similar vein to describe how painters of large villas solved the problem of wall decoration: "[They used] the varieties of landscape gardening, finding subjects in the characteristics of particular places; for they paint harbors, headlands, shores, rivers, springs, straits, temples, groves, hills, cattle, shepherds."

Painting of a seaside villa in the house of Lucretius Fronto, Pompeii. Paintings such as these opened up the walls of normally dark rooms with prospects that, in an ideal world, might have lain beyond them. (Stanley A. Jashemski)

Where there was no possibility—as in the town houses—of linking gardens architecturally with the wider landscape, Romans again resorted to illusion. To suggest that the garden was larger than in actuality it was, and to indicate that it was part of the larger landscape, property owners painted their garden walls. In a small house on the edge of Pompeii, a minute patch of ground had been made by filling a pool with soil. In the patch the owner made a modest flower bed, and to give the impression that it was part of a sizeable garden, he painted the rear and side walls of the enclosure. Sometimes there was no actual garden, only a painted one. On the wall of a light well in Herculaneum, in which nothing grew, there is a painting of a lattice fence, blooming oleanders, birds, and an *oscillum* (a hanging ornament) swaying in the breeze.

Paintings in the peristyle gardens were usually on the rear walls so that in axially planned houses, which ran directly from front to back, the painted garden would have been seen immediately on entering the house. The effect was to make the garden seem larger and the property grander. Slender Ionic columns painted on the walls of the gardens usually framed the view and suggested an extension of the porticoes along eastern and southern walls. To

Paintings on the south wall of the peristyle garden of the House of Venus, Pompeii. The side panels show gardens filled with flowers, ripening fruits, and birds. In the center panel, Venus, reclining on a large floating shell, is being wafted toward the garden; the effect is to erase the wall and open the view to the sea beyond. (Stanley A. Jashemski)

The west panel of the south garden wall, House of Venus, Pompeii. The plants in the foreground are identifiable — oleander, myrtle, and rose — but those beyond are indistinct. By drawing the eye into the picture, they seem to enlarge the actual garden. (Stanley A. Jashemski)

**Landscape with wild beasts on a garden wall in the house of Ceius Secundus, Pompeii. For Romans, the ideal habitat was one in which house, garden, and wider landscape were connected. (Stanley A. Jashemski)**

separate actual gardens from illusory ones, artists painted low wooden fences along the bottoms of the walls. But in some cases the line between the real and the unreal was deliberately blurred. In the house of L. Ceius Secundus, in Pompeii, water issuing from the basin of a painted fountain appears to empty into an actual gutter at the edge of the garden. In the same garden a painted border of myrtle and ivory plants, among which birds fly, continues the plantings of the real garden.

While some paintings merely extended the garden, others connected it to a landscape of fields, streams, hills, and sky. In some cases the background was a luxuriant estate furnished with well-stocked pools and lakes, beautiful gardens, and animal-filled parks. The idea of such estates had been

# Palace and Villa

brought to the West by Xenophon, who, on his famous march, had seen the great hunting parks of Persian kings and nobles. As well as protecting birds and other wild animals, the royal hunting parks were preserves for fruit trees, ornamental shrubs, and flowers. Xenophon named them *paradeisos*, after the Persian word *pardes*. When Alexander the Great conquered the Persians, he took possession of their *paradeisoi* and so liked them that on his return to the Mediterranean he created his own. When the Romans overran the Hellenistic world, they in turn acquired a taste for *paradeisoi*. Actual *paradeisoi* were beyond the means of most owners of villas and town houses, but all could afford to have pictures of them painted on their walls.

The Roman confidence in the world beyond the dwelling and, the corollary of this, the tendency to look outward rather than inward were further manifestations of the precocity of the classical world. The sense of house and garden, and of garden and landscape, as continuous spaces would not be matched for a millennium. In Roman Italy the human world and the natural world seem to have been in near-perfect accord. The house opened to the garden, and the garden, in the *villa urbana*, was a vestibule to a delightful and productive countryside. Distinctions between inside and outside were deliberately broken down, and where symbiosis was not physically possible, it was achieved by illusion.

# Cloister and Castle

Conditions that favor appreciation of landscape and the arts of gardening and decoration could not survive the collapse of Roman authority. Towns that were not destroyed or abandoned went into decline, and life shifted to a countryside that was neither controlled nor productive. Most of the barbarians knew nothing of urban life, and only those who had lived on the margins of the empire had seen gardens, orchards, or vineyards. According to French historians, England, Germany, and large parts of France, save for a few dismal agglomerations of buildings, were entirely without towns. Nature was all. In the disorder and insecurity that prevailed, the villa gave way to the castle, and both the castle and that other pillar of the early Middle Ages, the Church, turned their backs on landscape.

**MEDIEVAL WORLD VIEW**

The change in world view is demonstrated by roughly contemporaneous descriptions of a villa and two castles in Gaul. Built under the Pax Romana and in the spirit of Roman Italy, Appollinaris Sidonius's villa in the Auvergne enjoyed fine views of a lake and lay open to the sounds and sights of the pastoral landscape. By the sixth century, however, the barbarians were closing in, and the great uncertainty of life demanded stronger dwellings. In a poem, Sidonius described the castle of his friend Pontius Leontius, which stood high on the slope of a mountain above the confluence of the Garonne and the Dordogne. Around the building were walls and watchtowers and a defensive ditch.

The temper of the age is also reflected in Venantius Fortunatus's description of a castle, battlemented to withstand siege warfare, towering above the productive valley of the Moselle: "Here we see the vast frowning fortress, with the river below; the mighty towers contrasting with the peace of field and vineyard; the threatening ballista and the fruitful orchards."

This physical shunning of the world, as conditions deteriorated, was accompanied in Christian communities by a spiritual reorientation. Christian tutelage directed the eye away from the material world so that it might concentrate on the pressing concerns of the world of the spirit. In orthodox Christian circles pleasure in nature came to be regarded not simply as an irrelevance but as a pitfall on the road to salvation. Direct observation of nature had no place in official book learning. In art, which was in thrall to the Church, there was profound distrust of the sensory world and the untutored eye. Perspective and spatial relations were ignored or discarded. Figures, too, were distorted and backgrounds stylized as if to deliberately discount the world of primary perception in order to disclose the world of Christian truth. The setting of a painting served only to identify a figure or explain an action; a tree, for example, might have signified an outdoor scene, a corkscrew mountain a wilderness. Recognition, not representation, was the aim. The whole tendency of art was toward schematic abstraction: golden skies, decoratively disposed one-plane architecture, simplified tree forms. Whereas Roman wall paintings manifested a desire to look through the walls to the world beyond, Christian frescoes, by denying perspective and spatial relations, cast everything onto the surface of the wall.

Though the Church discouraged appreciation of natural beauty, it was, ironically, only in the monasteries and convents that settings were sufficiently architectural and life secure enough to allow the observation of nature. For monks and nuns, gratuitous satisfaction of the senses was taboo, but nature could be enjoyed as long as it was seen as emblematic of spiritual truths. Symbolism, therefore, offered a way out of the theological dilemma; through the pious contemplation of natural objects, a reflective man or woman might arrive at an intuitive understanding of God. Roses and lilies, which early Christians had condemned as heathenish flowers because they were Roman favorites,* were quickly brought under the wing of symbolism. Peter de Mora, cardinal archbishop of Capua, ascribed more than forty symbolic meanings to the rose. It was the choir of martyrs, or of virgins; when red, it was the blood of those who had died for the faith; when white, it was original purity. The lovely *Lilium candidum*, the Madonna lily, became a symbol for the purity of the Virgin. The cedar stood for humility, the cypress for piety, the palm for knowledge. Adam of St. Victoire, in a now well-known exercise, found in a nut a symbol of Christ: The green sheath is his Flesh, his Humanity; the shell is the body that hides his Godhead; and the kernel within, the sweet food of humanity, his Divinity.

**MONASTIC GARDENS**

As well as being the most advanced farmers of the Middle Ages, the monks were the leading ornamental gardeners. The monastic movement had begun in a garden: "I assembled in a garden [*hortus*] that Valerius had given me [at Hippo], certain brethren of like intentions with my own, who possessed nothing, even as I possessed nothing, and who followed after me." To this nucleus, thought to have been a villa with a peristyle garden, St. Augustine added a church and thereby established the elements of the monastic houses: buildings grouped around a quadrangle, or cloister. Around the sides of the cloister ran a covered walkway that protected the monks as they sat or walked. Monks are also known to have taken over derelict Roman properties, and these, too, may have influenced the form of the early monasteries. But whatever the precise origins of the form, the association of villa and cloister was so strong that even Jerome's monastery in Jerusalem, said to have been ascetic, was known as the "little villa of Christ."

The life of monastic communities centered on the cloister, where the monks gathered, meditated, and studied. To make the space pleasant, they turned it into an ornamental garden: a *jardin d'agrément* as opposed to a kitchen or an herb garden. By creating minor Edens the monks sanctified the space and at the same time prepared themselves for the heavenly gardens in the world to come. All gardens in the early Christian churches and monasteries are thought to have been paradisal reflections, and, so argue Derek Pearsall and Elizabeth Salter, few medieval authors used the word *paradise* without some sense of its full meaning. One wrote of a tenth-century cloister: "Before St. Mary's house [in the monastery at Reichenau] on the far side of the threshold is the garden, well-nursed, well-watered and lovely. About it there are walls, boughs swinging every way; it glows under

---

*Caligula walked to his bed over a carpet of red roses, and at Nero's banquets the scent of roses is said to have been overpowering.

the light like an earthly Paradise." Eventually, the name *paradise*—derived, through Xenophon and Greek, from the old Persian word for a hunting park and garden—became attached to the cloister garden and eventually to the entrance court of churches.

Monks delighted in their gardens. In the ninth century Adhelm, the bishop of Sherborne, with Virgil's *Georgics* at his side, versified on bees, and the young abbot Walafrid Strabo wrote yet another paeon (the poem *Hortulus*) to the beauty of the plants in the cloister of the monastery at Reichenau. The monastery is on an island in Lake Constance. Despite the Church's proscription, gardens evidently were a source of sensory satisfaction. Though flowers had medicinal and culinary uses, they were also grown for pleasure alone. Albertus Magnus, a thirteenth-century German Dominican monk, referred in his *De Vegetabilibus* to flowers in monastery gardens "intended for the pleasure of sight and smell." So fond did monks become of their gardens that guardians of the faith came to regard them as a dangerous diversion leading the faithful away from the path of virtue. In her book *Hortus Deliciarum* (Garden of Delights), the abbess Herrad of Landsperg told of a monk who had climbed to the very top of the ladder of Virtue but then looked behind him. Far below he beheld his flower garden and was seized by such a strong desire for it that he plunged headlong down because he had preferred the earthly to the heavenly paradise.

Women who adopted community life also perpetuated the Roman love of gardens and flowers. St. Radegund, wife of Clotaire I, who founded a convent at Poitiers in the sixth century to escape the dissolute life of the Merovingian court, almost always enclosed flowers with gifts of food she sent to the poet and churchman Venantius Fortunatus. At one meal for Fortunatus she covered the tablecloth with roses, placed wreaths on the dishes, and hung garlands on the walls, in the Roman fashion. Flowers were also used in the decoration of abbeys and even of monks. Abbeys then were decorated far more lavishly than they are today. On major feast days they were festooned with flowers; the monks wore crowns of flowers on their head and garlands around their neck.

In London on the annual feast day at St. Paul's it was customary for the dean and chapter to wear garlands of red roses. Church candles were wreathed with flowers, and floors were covered with sweet-scented rushes and herbs, such as mint and thyme. When Fortunatus was bishop of Poitiers, he urged that, "to remove the memory of fearful winter," churches be decorated with flowers and herbs in the spring: "When winter binds the earth with ice, all the glory of the field perishes with its flowers. But in the springtime when the Lord overcame Hell, bright grass shoots up and buds come

Medieval Italian miniature of a monk in his tree house or "roosting place" at one with birds, trees, and flowers. (By permission of the British Library)

forth. . . . Gather these first-fruits and . . . bear them to the churches and wreath the altars."

The practice of decorating abbeys and churches with flowers was not finally abandoned until the Reformation. When Roger de Walden was installed as bishop at St. Paul's Cathedral, in 1405, both he and the canons were decked with garlands of red roses. Flowers ultimately permeated the very core of the mass. Rosaries are so named because they were formed from a fragrant paste made from the crushed petals of rose leaves. So important did flowers become in the life of the Church that large churches and cathedrals routinely acquired gardens. Henry VI (reigned 1422–61) bequeathed to Eton College a piece of ground for the express purpose of growing flowers for the chapel. The floral garden was usually the sacristan's responsibility, but at some cathedrals there were also gardens for the prior and the canon. The sacristan's garden at Winchester is still called the paradise. That flowers were grown chiefly for the decoration of the church and the person is evident from their arrangement in the gardens; they were planted in ways that made them easy to pluck or cut, not to form pleasing assemblages.

**SECULAR GARDENS** In a near-wilderness dotted with castles and churches, affection for landscape, where it found expression at all, was narrowed to the confines of the garden. The monks may have preserved the body of the villa, but the Latin way of being related to the world had vanished. Until the twelfth century there were few ornamental gardens outside the monasteries, and most of these were restricted to castles and heavily fortified houses. Built primarily for domination and defense, on hilltops or else on plains where they were surrounded by wide moats, castles had little room for gardens. But even the most formidable fortresses—such as Chaucer's "Tour of gret myght"—were enlivened by a few flowers:

> About the tour was made a wall
> So that betwixt that and the tour,
> Roses were sette of swete savour,
> With many roses that they bere.

A castle or manor house with leftover space usually had a garden, known as the "orchard" or "pleasance," inside the walls or the moat. Invariably it, too, was enclosed—by a wall, a wooden palisade, or a thick hedge of hawthorn or quickset. The term *orchard* then referred to a turfed enclosure liberally studded with wildflowers, fruit trees, and shrubs. A typical orchard, according to the French garden historian Maumene, was a "somewhat disordered" place: a picturesque confusion of roses, hawthorns, and honeysuckles mixed with fruit trees and shrubs, all growing "in wild freedom." Flowers were not arranged in beds but grew promiscuously in the grass as if in imitation of natural meadows:

> Ful gay was all the ground and queynt,
> And poudred as men had it peynt,
> With many a fresshe and sondrie floure,
> That casten up ful good savour.

Boccaccio in the third day of the *Decameron* (1340–50) expressed the general delight with orchards: "What seemed more delightful than anything else was a plot of ground like a meadow, the grass of the deepest green, starred with a thousand various flowers." And in a fabliau (short story) of the twelfth and thirteenth centuries, the ideal pleasure garden was a flowery mead where a "thousand flowers, blue, yellow, white and red [over] the dark green tapestry in confusion spread." The orchard flowers were, of course, the lovely children of the meadow, not the improved flowers of later times.

On warm and sunny days orchards and pleasances were favored places where people played games, sang, danced, rested, and ate. On informal occasions they sat either on the sward or on seats of built-up soil, or planking, covered with turf. The seats were planted with short-stemmed flowers or with low-growing, aromatic herbs that gave off a pleasing aroma when crushed. So appealing were the pleasures of the garden that Crescentiis recommended, in 1305, that in royal gardens there should be a palace with rooms and towers made uniquely from trees where the lord and his lady might go in fine, dry weather.

Castles were dwellings as well as fortresses, and as the need for defense diminished, their residential functions became more important. During the twelfth and thirteenth centuries, halls and chambers replaced the gloomy donjons or keeps of many of the older, Norman castles. At Windsor, for example, Henry II (reigned 1154–89) built new royal lodgings, set about a quadrangle and an herb garden, on the north side of the upper bailey. In his last years at Arundel he ordered a garden to be made before his chamber window. At Windsor in 1236 glass was set in the windows of the queen's chamber which overlooked the garden, and at an early stage in the construction of the planned town and castle at Conway, a chamber, fronted by a lawn, was built for Queen Eleanor. The lawn was made with turf shipped up the river, fenced with the staves of an empty wine tun, and watered for the first time on a July evening in 1283 by Roger le Fykeys, one of the queen's esquires. Gentlewomen, who had been taught by the monks how to plant healing herbs, were the gardeners of the late Middle Ages, and gardens were usually located near their quarters.

King René d'Anjou in his garden house, from the book of hours of Isabella of Portugal, mid-fifteenth century. On the wall hangs a carpet, probably from the Levant; beyond the doorway is a walled medieval garden with box beds of herbs and flowers. (Bibliothèque Royale Albert, Brussels)

By the fourteenth century, castles were no longer mere refuges from attack (and bad weather) but centers of courtly life, surrounded by orchards
and gardens and frequently situated in tilled and cultivated countrysides. In
them developed a sophisticated appreciation of nature. To be at Senlis, Jean
de Jandun wrote in 1323, was "to be in gardens watered by running streams,
in flowery orchards and fertile herb gardens; to be in the wide meadows,
where the pleasant green of the springing grass and the fair diversity of brilliant flowers make a smiling picture for the eyes of men." A century earlier
Giraldus Cambrensis had been equally enchanted by Maenor Pyrr (now Man-
orbier), his family's castle in Pembrokeshire. The castle had a fish pond under its walls and a beautiful orchard enclosed on one side by a vineyard and
on the other by a wood remarkable for its projecting rocks and tall hazel trees.

**INTERIORS**

By present-day standards, castles and fortified
manor houses were cold, dark, and comfortless.
Floors at ground level usually were nothing more
than the natural soil well rammed down and cov-
ered with litter. Even when rammed, the surfaces were relatively soft, so
tables could be described as "fixed in the ground." The space below the dais,
or raised platform that held the high table, was often so foul, damp, and wet
that it was sometimes called the "marsh" of the hall. In houses, as in
churches, rushes were the usual coverings for floors of stone and tile, and
they remained so until the fifteenth century. In 1464 Sir John Howard paid
sixteen pence "to the gromys off chambre ffor rushis" for his parlor. In the
household of Edward IV (reigned 1461–70), it was the sergeant of the hall's
duty to see that rushes were supplied to the royal apartments. According to
the household book, the groom of the chamber was to bring daily "rushes
and litter for the paylettes all the yere." Jon the Gardener, in a poem written
in 1440, noted that lavender, wormwood, sage, hyssop, and rue were scattered over the floors of rooms to make them smell sweet. Herbs, for scenting,
and rushes were brought indoors by the custom of the jonchée. In the Middle
Ages a high smell lingered about any large habitation; kings cleared out
their castles from time to time, leaving the place bare in order "to sweeten
same."

Interiors were also decorated with flowers; Jon the Gardener mentions
the use of Madonna lilies and dried rose petals to sweeten damp and musty
rooms. In summer, Edward III's grooms were required to gather sweet herbs
and flowers to decorate and perfume the royal chamber: "The gromes shall
gadyr for the kinges gowns and shetes and othyr cloths the swete floures,
herbis, rotes, and thynges to make them breathe most holesomely and de-
lectable." Froissart described how in August 1391 the comte de Foix returned

to his room to find it covered with rushes and green leaves, roses, irises, and lilies of the valley; the walls were hung with boughs newly cut for perfume and coolness, as the weather was marvelously hot. In a poem written in 1312, Adam Davie Marshall described the marriage of Cleopatra thus:

> There was many a blithe grome
> Of olive and ruge floures,
> Weren ystrewed halle and boures,
> With samytes and bandekyns
> Weren curtayned the gardyns.

Flowers even entered the French Parliament. During the late spring when the roses of France were in fullest flower, it was the duty of particular peers to present a rose to each member of Parliament as he responded to a ceremonial roll call. For the occasion, the great chamber where Parliament met was transformed into a bower; vines and sprays of roses covered the walls, and pungent herbs sweetened the air.

In addition to seasonal or periodic intakes of herbs and flowers, all sizeable dwellings had permanent decorations. The chief exceptions were those castles and houses visited infrequently and for very short periods by peripatetic lords and monarchs. Interior stonework was usually whitewashed with a mixture of powdered chalk and water or plastered with a mixture of lime, sand, and hair. An especially fine, white plaster (French plaster or plaster of Paris) could be made by burning gypsum, which occurred in quantity near Montmartre. As in classical Italy, the plaster was smoothed and "polished" by thorough troweling. A third and more elaborate type of surface covering was wainscoting, whereby vertical boards of oak, or the more easily worked Norwegian fir, were laid over the stonework. Wainscot was a standard wall covering in the great houses of the thirteenth century.

The most common decorative practice was to paint both plastered and wainscoted surfaces. "Histories"—biblical incidents and scenes of battle and tournament—were the favored subjects, but by the beginning of the thirteenth century men of the knightly class were beginning to appreciate the beauty of flowers. Just as the flowers and leafage of the cloister garden had made their way into the abbey church, so the flowers and leafage of the castle garden entered castle halls and chambers. A popular form of decoration was to mark the whitewashed or plastered walls with lines, usually of red paint, to represent blocks of masonry, and within the blocks to paint flowers or foliage. In November 1238 the constable of the tower of London was instructed "to cause the walls of the queen's chamber . . . to be whitewashed and pointed, and within those pointings to be painted with flowers." Similar instructions were issued in February 1240: "The chamber of our queen in the aforesaid Tower [is to] be wainscoted without delay, and to be thoroughly whitened internally, and newly painted with roses." For models, the thirteenth-century decorators could have taken the trails of vine leaves and trefoils which then proliferated in the borders of the pages of illuminated Psalters and books of hours. These, according to Joan Evans, were the first cracks in the defenses of official, or symbolic, art; natural objects were perceived directly and, for the first time, portrayed with great accuracy.

From tentative beginnings with trails of leaves and sprays of flowers, decoration eventually encompassed trees and entire gardens. The objective, as in classical Italy, was to bring the beauty of the garden permanently within doors. Between 1350 and 1360, Charles v had the gallery of the queen's apartment in the Hotel Saint-Pol painted as a garden. The lower walls were painted with beds of lilies, roses, and other flowers, the upper with the trunks and branches of apple, pear, cherry, and plum trees. The branches soared into a vault that was painted blue and white to resemble sky. About fifty years later Jean sans Peur had the staircase of his Hotel de Bourgogne decorated with sculpted trees whose branches formed the ribs of the vaulted ceiling. A room in the castle of Chanze was painted all with gooseberry bushes, "dont les groyselles sont rouges."

**TAPESTRIES**

As well as being whitewashed and painted, walls were covered with hangings. In humbler dwellings, stained and painted cloths made by traveling painters or stainers were popular; stained cloths are thought to have been painted in distemper* or watercolors, painted cloths in oils. They were used as cheap substitutes for wall paintings and, more particularly, for woven and embroidered wall hangings. Painted cloths, which consisted of a canvas stretched on a wooden frame, seem to have had a longer vogue than stained; they were still used in inns and smaller mansion houses in the sixteenth century. "The English," wrote a French visitor in 1558, "make a great use of painted linens which are well done, and in which are magnificent roses." In the great houses, however, tapestry, in which the image was stitched and woven into the fabric itself, was the rule for hall and chamber by the fourteenth and fifteenth centuries.

The first tapestries and tapestry weavers in Europe are thought to have come from the eastern Mediterranean via southern France and Muslim Spain. In France and Flanders, woven hangings or coverings were known as Saracen work, *tapis sarrasinoys*, and in Germany and the Upper Rhine as heathen work, *heidnisch Werk*. By the thirteenth century, however, tapestry

---

*A type of paint in which the pigment is mixed with water and glue, or size.

weaving was a recognized European craft, and by the fourteenth it was practiced in countries as far apart as Spain and Sweden. For several centuries it
dominated the textile arts of Europe. Though a derived art, Focillon regarded it as an original expression of the European genius and the north's
answer to the Italian fresco. The first European tapestries are thought to
have been made in monastic workshops, with production then shifting to
the developing merchant towns as rising incomes and rising standards of
domestic comfort created a demand for household furnishings.

Two regions, both of precocious urban development, dominated production: Flanders and northern France. Paris was the first important center of
tapestry weaving, but it was quickly rivaled by the towns of the Scheldt
basin: Arras, Audenarde, Tournai, Bruges, and Brussels. Most of the Flemish towns made fine tapestries—"the people of Ypres color their wool with
skill and care," wrote Guillaume le Breton early in the thirteenth century—
but outside Flanders tapestry weaving was identified with a single town,
Arras, whose name became the generic term for tapestry.

The finest Flemish tapestries were made on high warp, or vertical,
looms, the weavers working from models, or cartoons, made either by the
weavers themselves or by professional painters. The cartoons were based on
original sketches or on miniatures from illustrated manuscripts enlarged to
the exact size of the tapestry. When reproducing the cartoons in wools and
silks, weavers usually made their own choice of colors and might even have
changed the details of the composition. Often, the cartoon was no more than
a graphic idea. When fresh, the finished cartoons, made from color washes
on thick paper or oils on linen, could be so attractive that they were sometimes used as substitutes for tapestries. Churches, for instance, were in the
habit of hanging only the cartoons, saving the actual tapestries for the great
fête days. Painted linens, known as *toiles peintes*, or *toiles de Bruges*, became
popular substitutes for tapestries and supported a specialist class of painters. In the will of Lady Hastings, dated 1503, there was a bequest of "an old
hangin of counterfeit Arras of Knollys, which now hangeth in the hall."

So great was the demand for tapestries that the merchants of Antwerp
and Bruges shipped them to all parts of Europe. Like spices, tapestries were
high priced and easily handled, indispensable attributes at a time when
transportation systems could not accommodate cheap and heavy goods.
England's imports date from at least as early as the mid-thirteenth century.
When Edward I reigned from 1272 to 1307, one of the chief duties of his
chamberlain was to make sure that the royal chambers were adorned with
hangings, "ut camerae tapetis et banqueiis ornentur." By the time of Henry V
(reigned 1413–22), even comparatively humble households had remarkable
lists of tapestries, and the inventories of royal and noble households ran to

# Cloister and Castle

several pages. Flemish tapestry weavers were prized immigrants, and to attract them to England, Edward III (reigned 1327–77) readily granted licenses and promised extraordinary privileges.

Most weavers set up their looms in towns, but in addition to stationary weavers there were groups of itinerants—*tapissiers de passage*–who formed part of that great company of mobile medieval laborers. They settled in places where new houses or churches were being built, or old ones refurbished, in the hope of being able to decorate them. Usually they took their looms to premises allocated by their patrons, and there, under the watchful eye of the patron, they made their tapestries.

In the houses of the prosperous, tapestries took the place of wall paintings. They were more sumptuous, and in cool, humid climates, they were also a more practical form of decoration. Thick woven wool panels, hung a foot or two from the walls, reduced drafts, prevented condensation, and were a barrier to the cold that stone walls store and radiate so effectively.* In dwellings, tapestries were first hung at the upper end of the hall to make sitting at the dais more comfortable. Comfort and decoration always started at, or above, the salt.

Tapestries were also used to decorate churches, but as solid Romanesque walls shrank before the onslaught of stained glass, hangings were relegated to the walls of the side aisles, hung over the stalls, or suspended between pillars. Castles and manor houses, however, remained fortresses until the end of the Middle Ages, and their walls, broken only by chimney breasts, narrow doors, and a few small, high windows, were ideal surfaces for the display of tapestries. By using pieces specially woven to hang between windows (*entre fenêtres*) or over doors (*portières*) it was possible to cover the entire wall surface.

Made from fabrics that were strong, flexible, and light enough to be loaded onto wagons or pack animals, tapestries were eminently moveable decorations. Army commanders carried them during campaigns so that they might line their tents. Tapestries were also an indispensable part of the baggage of the nomadic English and French nobility. The roads and rivers of England and France constantly bore the traffic of the great households. A special official of the suite of Anne of Brittany bore the title of "driver of the tapestry sumpter." In the course of the royal and noble migrations, tapestries were folded up, packed in coffers, loaded onto pack animals, and sent ahead to be set up in readiness for the arrival of their owners. The movements of King Charles VI (reigned 1380–1422) of France can be traced from

---

*The Association of Painters of Tapestry Cartoons, still extant in the 1950s, regarded tapestries as the best means of warming the cement walls of contemporary buildings.

sums in the royal account books laid out for the purchase of hooked nails, "tenter hooks," for hanging tapestries in the king's apartments. Monarchs continued to travel during the Renaissance: A Venetian ambassador to the court of Francis I (reigned 1515–47) testified that during the forty-five months of his embassy the court never stayed more than fifteen days in one place.

As well as lining walls, tapestries were placed on the backs of chairs and laid over benches, thus forming a kind of upholstery. Hung from rings, they were also used as partitions to divide into apartments the large, bleak halls of castles and manor houses. As moveable furnishings they could also be changed to suit particular moods, occasions, or seasons. During births, for example, rooms were often decorated with tapestries filled with flowers and birds. Rich households frequently bought sets for particular chambers or rooms. In 1467 the duke of Burgundy ordered from Pasquier Grenier, a tapestry merchant in Tournai, a "chamber" of four tapestries, all covered with shrubs and verdure and featuring peasants, woodcutting, plowing, and working in various manners. Charles V (1364–80) owned a beautiful green "chamber" of silk tapestries in which foliage designs lay on a green ground. Sir John Fastolf had scenes of hawking and hunting for autumn and of shepherds for summer. In addition to made-to-measure wall and doorway hangings, a "chamber" might include window curtains, cushion covers, and a canopy and covering for the bed.

For many centuries, too, tapestries were indispensable trappings for processions, feasts, and pageants. On feast days and festivals, fine cloths and tapestries were used to deck churches, and for processions and great occasions they were brought outdoors to set off the exteriors of houses. As they hung from windows and across the fronts of houses, the highlights of silk in the weave and gold and silver threads glinted in the sun. A finely decorated street was said to have been "well curtained." At Rheims, the coronation processions moved from the archbishop's palace to the cathedral between rows of walls covered with tapestries hung from windows and balconies. The entry of Elizabeth, wife of Henry VII, into London in 1486 was an equally brilliant spectacle: "Al the strets ther, whiche she shulde passe bye wer clenly dressed and besene with cloth of Tappestrye and Arras; and some streetes as Chepe, hanged with riche clothes of golde, velvettes and silkes."

**TAPESTRY SUBJECTS**     *The Chase.* As in wall paintings, scenes of battle and tournament and incidents from myth, legend, and the Bible were the most popular subjects, but the inventories of noble houses also listed large numbers of tapestries devoted to the life, labors, and pleasures of the countryside. If women came to an awareness of nature through the garden, and the fields and meadows that lay immediately beyond it, men of the knightly class, speaking generally, became aware of it through the chase. Castles, manor houses, and towns were surrounded by meadows, woodland, and unenclosed fields in which the lords and burghers, and even their wives, might hunt at will. For kings and courtiers vast forests were maintained expressly for the exercise of the noble art, and fearsome penalties were exacted upon intruders.

To some extent, hunting in the Middle Ages was still a matter of stocking the larder. Meat was an important commodity, venison in particular, and certain animals were dangerous: the boar and the bear to people, and the otter to fish. But in royal and aristocratic circles hunting needed no justification. It was at once a sport, an art, and, for those of a certain temper, a compelling ritual engaged in for its own sake. It was the first nonutilitarian use of wild nature. Tracking the beast to its haunts, knowing its habits, caring for and training the hounds, learning the terms of venery, and being initiated into such exquisite matters as the undoing or "gralloching" of the deer were deemed arts of the highest order. The dead beast was cut up according to strict protocol and with great ceremony, the hunters, in their varying degrees, and the dogs getting particular parts of the carcase. To appreciate the finer points of the ceremony, and to dissect the beast without bloodying even one's sleeves, was to be truly noble.

Some were so possessed by the chase that it was said of them that they would sooner hunt than eat. Hunting took up most of their time and all of their energy. Some, too, would sooner hunt than fight. Frederick of Hohenstaufer, king of Sicily and Germany (reigned 1212–50), once broke off a siege to indulge in a day's hunting. Equally zealous was Gaston Phébus, comte de Foix and lord of Bearn, who, a few years before his death—on a bear hunt in the woods of Sauveterre in 1391—wrote the most famous of all medieval hunting books: *Le livre de chasse* (1387/89). In it he declared that hunters were the healthiest and happiest of men. Thoroughly preoccupied, they were free of "mauveises ymaginations et pensementz" and when they returned home in the evening they washed "par aventure tout le corps," and so to bed "sanz penser de fere pechiez." He also believed that as well as leading more carefree lives than other men, hunters, in quiet moments before the start of the hunt, saw the world with new eyes: the sweet and fair morn, the melodious song of small birds, and the fresh dew upon twigs and grasses. Often, too, huntsmen acquired an acute and sympathetic understanding of the animals hunted. The most lifelike scenes in the borders of the Bayeux Tapestry* are those of the chase.

---

*Technically, the Bayeux Tapestry is an embroidery. The images were sewn onto a linen ground.

*Peasants Hunting Rabbits with Ferrets.* Franco-Burgundian, ca. 1450–75, possibly from the looms of Pasquier Grenier, a prominent tapestry merchant and manufacturer from Tournai. Hunting, even of small game, was a subject of the greatest interest. The tapestry shows the preparatory stages of the rabbit hunt: sharpening a peg, taking a ferret from its basket, laying the nets over the rabbit holes, and restraining the dogs on the leash. (Burrell Collection, Glasgow Museums and Art Galleries, with permission)

So great was the interest in hunting that scenes of the chase passed from books on hunting into every field of decorative art. When rough weather kept hunters indoors, they liked nothing better than to have reminders of their pleasures about them. Hunting scenes were popular subjects for painted tiles, frescoes, tapestries, and easel paintings. The frescoes in the garderobe (dressing room) of the Palace of the Popes at Avignon, painted about 1350 and showing scenes of hunting, hawking, fowling, and fishing, were meant to turn the room into a forest glade. Inventories attest to the popularity of hunting

*Hunting the Deer*, 1425–50; one of the Devonshire Tapestries. In the center foreground, the deer is being undone, or "gralloched." As in medieval paintings, perspective is rudimentary; the richly clad figures climb up the surface of the tapestry rather than recede into its depths. Stag hunting in the Middle Ages was an exclusively aristocratic sport. (By courtesy of the Board of Trustees of the Victoria & Albert Museum)

tapestries, sometimes listed as "forest" and "park" work, but relatively few have survived.

One of the most celebrated sets was found (in 1899) cut into strips and nailed in the bays between the windows of the long gallery of Hardwick Hall, a house owned by the dukes of Devonshire. The tapestries may well have been the same "tapestrie hanginges with personages of forrest worke of fyftene foote and a half deep" listed in a 1601 inventory of the property. Six pieces were listed: four in the great entrance hall and two in "My Ladie's Bed Chamber." "My Lady" was the redoubtable Bess of Hardwick, countess of Shrewsbury, builder of Hardwick Hall and custodian of Mary Stewart of Scotland. The set now consists of four very large hangings, each about 14 feet high and 35 feet long. Size alone would distinguish them (they are in fact the largest surviving images of any kind from the fifteenth century), but they are also, according to Donald King, former keeper of textiles at the Victoria and Albert Museum, the most ambitious representations of contemporary life in that age. King also believed that the designers of the cartoons were influenced by the miniatures in the *Livre de chasse* of the comte de Foix. Woven in Flemish workshops between 1425 and 1450, the Devonshire tapestries are a record of hunting and hawking practices in the first half of the fifteenth century. They showed how waterfowl were beaten up from the streams, how the falcon was flown, the lure displayed, and the bird recaptured. Falcons in the fifteenth century were used to bring down wild geese. Other panels show hunts of the stag and the heron, the otter and the swan, and the bear and the boar. Otters were coveted for their skins, and swans were an important item in the medieval diet. The wild boar, the most dangerous of all the animals of the chase, was hunted on foot with short jobbing spears and with the help of those standard accompaniments to the medieval hunt—lithe hounds of the greyhound type.

Unlike the modern hunt, the medieval chase was not an equestrian exercise. Horses are not mentioned in books on the chase, and, as Derek Pearsall has pointed out, a medieval rider would have been as surprised as his horse if expected to jump a gate or a fence. The greatest and most aristocratic sport was hunting the stag "by force of hounds," or simply "parforce." Two kinds of hounds were used, those that ran by scent and those (wolfhounds and greyhounds) which coursed by sight. A large part of the pleasure and excitement of the hunt lay in the "bruit," the sound of baying dogs. For Gace de la Buigne, a fourteenth-century chaplain to the kings of France, the "bruit" was the music of heaven: "When the hounds give tongue, never has man heard melody to this. No Alleluia sung in the chapel of the king is so beautiful . . . as the music of the hunting hounds." He was also enraptured by the "prise" or "mort," sounded on the horn to signal the death of a deer: "No man who hears such a melody would wish for any other paradise."

*Country Labors and "Verdures."*   Hunting may have brought the most vital contact with the countryside, but people also rode in nearby woods and meadows for sheer delight. After a winter confined to a castle, manor house, or tightly packed, gray-walled town, the warmth, color, and fragrance of the spring and summer landscapes were intoxicating. "And I wish that all times were April and May," ran a thirteenth-century lyric, "and every month renew all fruits again and every day fleurs-de-lis and gillyflowers and violets and roses wherever one goes, and woods in leaf and meadows green." Pero de Niño, a Spanish knight who visited Normandy about 1405, described a cavalcade of knights and ladies who rode through the country making chaplets of flowers, singing lays and ballads, and in the afternoons hawking by the river and picnicking in the meadows.

There are similar scenes in the *Tres riches heures* (1416), a book of devotional texts, exquisitely illustrated with scenes from rural life, commissioned by Jean, duc de Berry. In the illustration, or illumination, for May a cavalcade of knights and ladies, garlanded with fresh green leaves, rides out to meet the spring morning, caroling as they go: "C'est le mai, c'est le mai,

*Sheepshearing*, Tournai, ca. 1475. An idealized view of rural life and labor. (Institut Royal du Patrimoine Artistique, Brussels)

c'est le joli mois de mai." Elsewhere, the prince and poet Charles D'Orleans was singing: "Time has shed its cloak / of wind rain and cold / to assume the embroidery of the sun / shining bright and beautiful."

As they picnicked in the woods and meadows, or rode to the chase, knights, burghers, and their ladies looked with romantic envy at plowmen, shepherds, and woodcutters. Life in the courts, castles, and burgeoning towns had become sophisticated enough for people to feel a sentimental yearning for rural life. Labors of the months, which until the fourteenth century had been tied to calendar settings, became subjects for independent decorative schemes. Scenes of sowing, plowing, pruning, threshing, and sheep shearing began to appear in wall paintings and tapestries.

As hunting shifted from the open countryside to forests where game was protected by law, interest in the life of the woods increased noticeably. Woodcutters sawing, piling logs, and loading carts became popular subjects for tapestries. With time, the woods became interesting for their own sake. In the Avignon hunting frescoes the forest background is as important as the figures of the hunters, and by the end of the Middle Ages the forest could stand alone; it needed neither fowler nor falcons, woodsman, huntsman, nor

*The Woodcutters*, Tournai, 1450–75. As hunting shifted from open countryside to the forest, interest quickened in the life of the woods. Here woodsmen are shown sawing and piling logs and loading them into carts. (Musée des Arts Décoratifs, Paris; all rights reserved)

hounds. People, animals, and buildings were allowed into the "verdures" or "wilderness tapestries," but they never dominated. Pride of place belonged to the branches, leaves, and flowers, and usually they were rendered very carefully. Of the hundred or so plants represented in the *Hunt of the Unicorn* tapestries, now in the Cloisters of the Metropolitan Museum in New York, botanists have been able to identify eighty-five.

Designers and weavers were not only extravagant about varieties of plants, but they were also seldom punctilious about seasons of flowering. A tree might bear ripe cherries while daffodils bloomed, and hawthorns blossom while holly was in berry. Each plant was usually represented in its prime so that nature in the tapestries, like nature in the garden of Alcinoüs, was often more bountiful and varied than the nature we see. It was also more colorful. The brilliant reds and greens have now faded to purples and yel-

*The Noble Pastoral: The Preparation of Wool*, Loire, early sixteenth century. A "millefleurs" tapestry in which the figures, characteristically, are foils for the true subject — the floral background. (Cliché des Musées Nationaux, Paris, © Photo R.M.N.)

lows, but in their prime the tapestries were resplendent. Yet a woven ideal was, of course, no substitute for an actual landscape. When Pantagruel and his friends visited the Land of Satin, where the trees and herbage never lost their leaves or flowers, they were disappointed. The birds did not sing, and when the narrator plucked the fruit hanging from the tapestries, "there was no morsel of savour in them."

A variation of the standard verdure or wilderness tapestry was the small verdure or "millefleurs," so called because the figures were placed in settings filled with flowers. The foreground of many a late medieval or Gothic tapestry was sprinkled with the loved common flowers of the field and the wood. Flowers even obtruded into battle scenes, between the feet of the warriors and the hooves of the horses. Occasionally weavers were so captivated by them that they would produce nothing but lily bells, cowslips, daisies, rosemary, and rue. As in the verdures proper, figures might be allowed into the composition, but usually they were mere foils for the blue or dark pink backgrounds powdered with innumerable sprays of tiny wildflowers. These were mingled as though on the floor of a pleasance or a natural meadow. The precursor of the millefleurs tapestry might well have been a sheet covered with posies of actual flowers. On "Fête Dieu" (the Feast of Corpus Christi) the streets of French country towns are still decorated with sheets to which posies of flowers have been pinned; and when Pope John Paul II entered Warsaw in 1979, carpets pinned with flowers were hung from windows.

Historians of decoration and design usually consider the late medieval or Gothic tapestries to have been ideal wall coverings. Until the arrival of steel framing and reinforced concrete, a basic principle of decoration was that the flatness or solidity of the wall not be sacrificed. The wall supported the ceiling, and though people may never have considered this, they were aware of it unconsciously. Perspectives and prospects that appeared to pierce the wall violated its mechanical integrity, even though, as in Roman wall paintings, this may have been restored to some extent by painted pillars. The vertical accents of the Gothic tapestries gave the feeling of a supporting construction; figures and buildings tend to climb one on top of the other instead of receding into the depths of the picture. By ignoring the laws of vision, Gothic tapestries also enhanced the sense of privacy and—crucial in the Middle Ages—the sense of shelter; realism, by being too intrusive, may have dispelled these illusions. A final attribute, which applies chiefly to the verdures and millefleurs tapestries, is that they were exceptionally well balanced; no one element stood out. This meant—an unintended bonus—that they could be cut up almost at will, partly hidden by a mirror or a painting, or interrupted by an angle in the wall without any loss of decorative effect.

# Renaissance House and Garden

istories of the house usually place the dawn of comfort in the fourteenth and fifteenth centuries. The revival of commerce, the revitalization of the towns, and increases in the supply of money made possible better houses and more elaborate fittings and furnishings. The changes were felt first in Italy. When Charles VIII of France traveled overland to claim his kingdom in Naples in 1495, he and his young companions were intoxicated by the beauty of the towns, the suburban villas, and the ornamental gardens. The wave of their joy crested in Naples itself. "You cannot believe what wonderful gardens I have seen in this town," wrote Charles, "for on my word, it seems as though only Adam and Eve were wanting to make an Earthly Paradise, so full are they of rare and beautiful things." Charles' enthusiasm was echoed by Cardinal Briconnet: "The king in his gracious favour has been pleased to show me everything, both inside and outside the city. And I assure you that the beauty of the palaces is incredible, with the furnishings of this world's pleasures in every possible kind."

One palace in particular captivated the French sojourners: the beautiful villa Poggio Reale, designed fifteen years earlier by the architect Serlio as a summer residence for the crown prince Alfonso. Charles' own castle at Amboise was a typical medieval fortress replete with corner towers, crenellations, and encircling walls. Serlio, who had been guided by Lorenzo de' Medici, revived classical canons of architecture by turning the building outward to the landscape rather than inward to a court. Windows and loggias let in light and air and brought the building into relation with the gardens that surrounded it and the lovely countryside that lay beyond. The days of fortresslike buildings, which Leon Battista Alberti had found "altogether inconsistent with the peaceable Aspect of a well governed City or Commonwealth," were numbered. New country houses in Italy, after the fashion of the ancients, would be points from which the eye, as Serlio recognized, might range over "pleasant Landskips, flowery Meads, open Champains, shady Groves, [and] limpid Brooks."

**TUDOR HOUSES**    From Italy the practice of unfolding buildings and bringing them into relation with the surrounding countryside spread to France, the Low Countries, and England. Northern houses and gardens would not match the openness and splendor of the Italian for at least a century, but at the time of Charles' Italian journey medieval enclosures were beginning to come down. In England, the accession of the Tudors, which finally ended the Wars of the Roses, brought relative peace to a war-torn countryside. Energy and resources that formerly had been spent on defense could now be directed at the house. Castles and heavily fortified houses, which had been little more than refuges, were made obsolete by effective artillery and, more particularly, by a law-abiding countryside. Their replacements were lighter, more open buildings, frequently built of brick and situated on low rather than high ground. John Leland, an antiquary as well as a surveyor to Henry VIII (reigned 1509–47), noted the changes as he traveled through the countryside: "The old house of the Chenies is so translated by my Lord Russell . . . that little or nothing of it in a manner remaineth untranslated, and a great deal of the house is even newly set up, made of brick and timber, and fair lodgings [probably a banqueting house] be new erected in the garden."

Yet in the northern countries the ways of the Middle Ages were given up slowly. New houses were still given a coping of conventional battlements, which were often more ostentatious than functional, and surrounded by a stream-fed moat. In short, they were houses capable of withstanding a moderate assault, not fortresses. The historian Francis Grose described the tran-

# Renaissance House and Garden

sition in 1773: "Our nobility and gentry built themselves more pleasant and airy dwellings, relinquishing these ancient, dreary mansions of their forefathers, where the enjoyment of light and air was sacrificed to the consideration of strength, and whose best rooms, according to our modern refined notions have more the appearance of gaols and dungeons for prisoners than apartments for the reception of a rich and powerful baron."

In older buildings, walls were pointed, crevices repaired, and chimneys, fireplaces, and glazed windows added to existing halls and apartments. Open, chimneyless fires and those enemies of decoration, soot and smut, were no longer tolerated. Chaucer's telling description (1386) of the Nun's Priest's dwelling—"Fful sooty was hir bour and eek hire halle"—would find no echo in Elizabethan poetry. The great, cavernous halls were also made more liveable; second stories were inserted, and both upper and lower floors were divided into rooms. In some of the larger Tudor houses, entire upper-story walls were filled with windows to form "long galleries" that overlooked the lawns and knots of the gardens. New Hardwick Hall, built in the late sixteenth century, was described as a building with "more glass than wall." Women, who seldom went out of doors during the winter months, used the bright galleries for taking gentle exercise and for sewing, embroidery, and other household pursuits.

Glass, however, remained a luxury until the seventeenth century. Windows were regarded as part of the furnishings of a room, not of the fabric of the house. Glass casements were moveable chattels until 1579—"for without glass," read Lord Coke's report to Elizabeth I, "is no perfect house"—and they were frequently bequeathed. So valuable were windows that when householders were absent, they were usually removed and carefully laid by. In very old houses, grooves may still be seen in the stonework of the windows where the frames that contained the glass were fitted in. Oiled cloth and paper, shaved horn, and mica frequently substituted for glass, but the standard window covering was the wooden shutter. Not until the end of the sixteenth century was glass plentiful enough that horn could be "quite laid downe," and even then glass was more frequently translucent than transparent.

**TUDOR GARDENS**   There were also great changes in the aspects of houses and in the gardens that surrounded them. Though gardens were still enclosed, their owners had begun to dispense with high, castellated walls and impenetrable hedges. Latticework fences sometimes replaced walls, and plants more ornamental than the thorn—yew, privet, or sweetbriar—were used for hedging. By the middle of the fifteenth century in England, gardens

*The Franklin Hanging*, English embroidery, late sixteenth century. A fine mansion house and garden, with mazes, elaborate pavilions, and a fountain. Beyond the garden is a hunting park and open countryside. (By courtesy of the Board of Trustees of the Victoria & Albert Museum)

were no longer the preserve of religious houses and landed nobility. The average country squire had a modest garden attached to his house, as did the yeoman.

By the sixteenth century, the pleasure garden—Gervase Markham's "garden for flowers and sweet smells" or Olivier de Serres's "nosegay garden"—was beginning to challenge the ascendancy of the herb or vegetable garden. The beauty of Elizabethan gardens, remarked historian William Harrison in 1577, had been "wonderfully increased . . . so that in comparison . . . the ancient gardens were but dunghills. Harrison continued: "How art also helpeth nature in the daily colouring, doubling and enlarging the proportion of our flowers, it is incredible to report; for so curious and cunning are our gardeners now in these days that they presume to do in manner what they list with nature and moderate her course in things as if they were her superiors." When John Parkinson wrote his much loved *Paradisi in sole Paradisus Terrestris* in 1629, the herb or vegetable garden had been relegated to the side or rear of the house: "for the many different sents that arise from the herbes, as cabbages, onions etc. are scarce well pleasing to perfume the lodgings of any house." Flowers that kept company with onions and parsnips suffered, wrote William Lawson in 1617, "some disgrace."

So cherished were gardens that they were held to be only slightly less important than the houses themselves. It was customary for the designer of the house also to design the garden. Richard Surfleet, in *The Countrie Farme* (1600), described his joy at looking over his garden and seeing "fair and comely proportions, handsome and pleasant arbours, and as it were closets, delightful borders of lavendar, rosemary, box and other such like." He was also pleased to be able to smell "so sweet a nosegay so near at hand." Fynes Moryson wrote, in 1617, "There is no countrie . . . where all sorts of men allot so much ground about their houses for the pleasure of garden and orchards." Without gardens, wrote Lord Bacon in his celebrated essay (*Of Gardens*, 1625), "buildings and palaces are but gross handiworks: and a man shall ever see that when ages come to civility and elegancy, men come to build stately sooner than to garden finely;—as if gardening were the greater perfection."

Not only were the new gardens larger and more open than the old, but they were markedly different in form as well. The usual surround for a Tudor garden was a leafy tunnel supported by a framework of wooden trellises called "carpenter's work." Within the trellises beds were arranged symmetrically, and they were brought into relationship with the house by main walks or "forthrights" that were aligned with the house's main axes. The beds themselves were defined by lines of clipped low hedges, or "knots," of dwarf shrubs and herbs such as box, lavender, hyssop, thyme, and rosemary. Knots, which could be geometrical or free flowing, were so called because they resembled the patterns that could be made with knotted cord. The spaces between the knots were filled with flowers—primroses, sweet williams, carnations, and violets—or, as in the case of the French *potager*, with vegetables. The knots became so intricate that later they were sometimes made solely for their patterns. In such cases, the earth between the knots was left bare or covered with turf or colored sands and gravels. To give the beds extra sparkle, the filling was sometimes pieces of ground glass.

Knotted beds were popular for more than two centuries. The designs were of lasting interest, and the varied shades of the dwarf evergreen shrubs provided some color in winter. Without winter-flowering heaths and early-flowering species of crocus and iris, flowers were few from the time the hollyhocks faded in late summer till the first snowdrops appeared in January or February. Knots, as Shakespeare put it, were "the flowers of winter." So that their patterns and colors might be seen to advantage, they were usually placed below the long galleries or the windows of apartments, which were normally on the second floor. In Henry VIII's privy gardens, for example, the

An embroidered valance, ca. 1600, showing a garden, country labors, and a fruitful late-summer countryside — features in which all Elizabethans rejoiced. (All rights reserved, The Metropolitan Museum of Art. Gift of Irwin Untermyer, 1964 [64.101.1280])

knots lay immediately below the king's apartments. The knots could also be seen from raised terraces and artificial mounds, "mounts," within the garden. But not everyone thrilled to the sight of knots. Francis Bacon found them tasteless: "[They were] but Toys: you may see as good Sights many times in Tarts."

Tudor gardens gave such delight that in fine weather all social activity gravitated to them. They were the scene for masques and revels, music and dancing, eating and entertaining, and sports and games of all kinds. Eleanour Rohde, the English garden historian, found that gardens and orchards served as settings for twenty-nine Shakespearean scenes. Some sense of the spell they cast is evident in Stephen Hawe's verse, written in 1509:

> Then in we wente to the garden gloryous,
> Like to a place of pleasure most solacyous
> Wyth Flora paynted and wrought curyously,
> In divers knottes of marvaylous gretenes.

As decorative extensions of the house, gardens were dressed to match the mood of the entertainments. With "carpenter's work," amazing transformations could be achieved overnight and all manner of theatrical effects created. Skilled gardeners and handymen could easily make outdoor "rooms" that resembled the chambers, and even the long galleries, of Elizabethan houses. High green hedges spangled with blossoms or trelliswork hung with greenery and flowers substituted for tapestries, and quaint topiary shapes for high-standing furniture.

All sizeable gardens also had permanent and semipermanent structures for reading and relaxation, dining, and entertaining. The most ingenious were arbors made out of growing trees. Surplus branches were cut from the tree and the remainder trained to make a room several feet above ground level. Upper branches bent down and around formed the roof and sides of the

Detail (of above). The alley in carpenter's work — which replaced the medieval wall — provided shade, privacy, and a frame for the garden, here divided into four square plots. Elizabethan and Jacobean gardens were settings for music and dance.

room; the lower boughs, often buttressed by extra supports pushed in from below, supported a floor made of planking. Some tree arbors were mere roosting places where one could read or write a book, but others were elaborate. In Holland and England, the horizontal boughs of lime trees supported arbors that were sometimes two and even three stories high. Parkinson in his *Paradisus* described a three-story arbor so roomy that there was space for at least fifty people in each of the first two stories:

> And I have seen at Cobham in Kent, a tall or great bodied Lime Tree, bare without boughes for eight foote high and then the branches were spread round so orderly, as if it were done by art, and brought to compasse the middle Arbour: and from those boughes the body was bare again for eight or

A surviving tree house at Pitchford Hall, Shropshire. It is smaller in scale than the Tudor dining arbors but large enough to require support from below. The half-timbered exterior dates from the late eighteenth century, but the framework is much older. (Courtesy, Royal Commission on the Historical Monuments of England)

nine foote (wherein might be placed halfe a hundred men at the least, as there might be likewise in that underneath this) & then another rowe of branches to encompasse a third Arbour, with stayres made for the purpose to this and that underneath it: upon the boughes were laid boards to tread upon, which was the goodliest spectacle mine eyes ever beheld for one tree to carry.

Many French, Italian, and English gardens also had summer houses and pavilions, made from brick or stone, which were used for banquets and as

# Renaissance House and Garden

places where the women of the household might sit and sew or listen to music. In Tudor England large garden houses with towers, turrets, and chimney pots were so fashionable that a contemporary chronicler rebuked their owners for squandering money that might otherwise have been spent on hospitals and alms houses. Banqueting houses were also made for special occasions, and to give them an appearance of permanency, they were decorated with ivy and evergreens. Stow, in his *Annals* for 1581, described a banqueting house at Whitehall made for the entertainment of "certaine Ambassadors out of France." The circular house, 332 feet around, "was wrought most cunningly with ivy and holly, with pendants made of wicker rods garnished with bay, rue, and all manner of strange flowers garnished with spangles of gold . . . beautiful with teasons [festoons] made of ivy and holly." The building was roofed with canvas painted to look like a summer sky.

So persistently did indoors and outdoors echo each other that the effect, as Barnaby Googe noted with some enthusiasm in 1577, could be delightfully ambiguous: "Your parlers and your banketting houses, both within and without, are all bedecked with pictures of beautiful Flowres and Trees, that you may not onley feede your eyes with the beholding of the true and lively flowre, but also delight your selfe with the counterfaite in the middest of Winter."

Gardens were popular in towns as well as in the country. In *Utopia* (1516), Sir Thomas More envisaged strife and contention between the inhabitants of rival streets over the trimming, husbanding, and furnishing of their gardens. Most Tudor towns had orchards, closes, and gardens in which well-to-do inhabitants grew—in addition to fruit, herbs, and vegetables—flowers for "delight and ornament." In crowded areas people sometimes made small gardens in the streets alongside the walls. Londoners were garden lovers as early as the reign of Edward I (from 1272 to 1307), when a nursery trade supplied trees, flowering plants, and turf ready for laying. In the seventeenth century John Worlidge noted that there was "scarce an Ingenious Citizen that by his confinement to a Shop, being denied the privilege of having a real Garden, but hath his boxes, pots or other receptacles for Flowers, Plants, etc." Failing this, the town dweller had at the very least a flower painting on his or her wall, drawn "to satisfye the fancy of such that either cannot obtain the Felicity of enjoying them in Reality, or to supply the defect that Winter annually brings."

In *Floraes Paradise* (1608), Sir Hugh Platt instructed Londoners on the design of window boxes: "In every window you may make square formes either of lead or of boards well pitched within; fill them with some rich earth and plant with flowers or hearbs therin as you like best." For the decoration of doorways he suggested sweetbriar and rosemary, while the chimney piece, in summer, "may be trimmed with a fine bank of mosse or with aspen . . . or the white flower called everlasting. And at either end Rosemary pots."

Though the pleasures of gardens were peerless, people also delighted in the countryside. John Stow described how on May Day Elizabethan Londoners "would walk into the sweet meadows and green woods, there to rejoice their spirits with the beauty and savour of sweet flowers, and with the harmony of birds." For Elizabethan poets and playwrights the spring and summer landscapes were a rich and regularly replenished source of images. Where else in literature, asked Eleanour Rohde, can one gather such handfuls of flowers as in the works of the Elizabethans? In Shakespeare alone she found sixty passages "fragrant" with roses. The favorite season was spring, "the sweet of the year" and "the year's pleasant king," and the favorite month "proud-pied April, dress'd in all his trim." Winter, by contrast, was a hideous season of dark days and tedious nights fit only for the telling of sad tales. Thomas Nashe's censure, in 1592, went even deeper than Shakespeare's: "From winter, plague and pestilence the good Lord deliver us."

Though spring and summer were joyful seasons, the flowering, not yet extended by plant importations from the Middle East, China, and Japan, was short and, by present-day standards, relatively subdued. In the sixteenth century roses were finished by midsummer—thus the great popularity of "July-flowers": pinks, carnations, or "gillyflowers," to give them their Elizabethan name. There were fewer varieties of flowers than we are now accustomed to, and all were much smaller—more like flowers in an Alpine meadow than in a florist's shop. Even the "nosegay" flowers, cultivated in gardens for their sweet scent, could scarcely be distinguished from the "spontaneous finery," as Maurice Maeterlinck described English wildflowers in 1905, "of [the] woods and of [the] snow-frightened, wind-frightened fields."

But the flower garden's loss, due to the shortness of the flowering season, was the orchard's gain. Orchards were doubly appreciated in the fall for their harvest of fruits and their late-season beauty. For Ralph Austen, author of *A Treatise of Fruit Trees* (1653), vineyards and orchards ranked with the "Flowers, Starres and Paradises of the Earth." The orchard, he opined, was a cornucopia for all the senses—sight, smell, taste, and, not least, feel: "Some [of the fruits are] as soft as silke and some as prickly as an Hedgehog." Orchards, too, were havens for small birds, which though still devoured in great numbers, had by the seventeenth century become objects of affection. A brood of nightingales, William Lawson wrote in 1617, "graced" an orchard. In addition to being delightful company, nightingales, Lawson noted, also helped to "cleanse . . . trees of caterpillars and all noysome worms and flies."

# Renaissance House and Garden

**INTERIORS**

Throughout the early modern period, the practice of bringing plant material indoors continued unabated. Yew and box, Parkinson noted, were used "to deck up houses in the winter-time." Flowers were still grown chiefly as raw material for medicines and perfumes, but by Tudor times many gardens had plots devoted entirely to the growing of nosegays. Single sprigs and posies, held in the hand or pinned near the face beside their embroidered counterparts, appear over and over again in Elizabethan portraits; women, too, wore chaplets or garlands on their persons. Nosegays were also placed in bedrooms, and in summer boughs, wreaths, and flowers were spread over hearths and mantels. In 1595 Lord Montague told his yeoman of the wardrobe that all galleries and lodgings reserved for strangers were to be "cleanly and sweetly kepte, with herbs, flowers and bowes in their seasons." Madonna lilies and dried rose petals, sometimes powdered and mixed with spices, were used for scenting damp and musty rooms. The practice of keeping potpourri in parlors and bedrooms became so widespread that English gardens could not supply enough petals; dried yellow roses from Constantinople became a recognized import.

The English method of decorating rooms greatly pleased Levimus Lemnius, a young Dutchman who visited England in 1560: "Their chambers and parlours strawed over with sweet herbes refreshed mee; their nosegays finely intermingled with sundry sorts of fragraunte flowers, in their bed chambers and privy rooms, with comfortable smell cheered me up, and entirely delighted all my senses." Lemnius also noted that succulent green foliage, being cooler than straw, mitigated heat: "It shall be very good to sprinkle the pavements and cool the floors of our houses and chambers with the springing water and then strew them over with sedge, and to trimme up our parlours with green boughs, fresh herbs and vine leaves; which thing . . . no nation [does] more decently, more trimmely, nor more sightly than . . . Englande." Houses, like churches, were also decorated at the major religious festivals:

> When yew is out, and birch comes in,
> And many flowers beside
> Both of a fresh and fragrant kind
> To honour Whitsuntide,
> Green rushes then, and sweetest bents
> With cooler open boughs,
> Come in for comely ornaments
> To re-adorn the house.
>     (Robert Herrick, "Candlemas Eve")

Floors were still covered with rushes or bents (coarse dried grass) which were sprinkled or "strewn" with flowers and gathered herbs and with clippings from the pungent herbs of the knots. In France, the depth of the floor cover was a measure of wealth: A very rich person was "dans la paille jusques le ventre," waist deep in straw. Nearly two dozen varieties of herbs were considered suitable for strewing. John Parkinson noted, in *Theatrum Botanicum* (1660), the demand for germander and hyssop, "being pretty and sweet," as "strewing" herbs for houses. To clear the fetid air in his chambers at Hampton Court, Cardinal Wolsey—who is said to have held his nose even when crossing his own courtyard—used to cover the floors with rushes strongly impregnated with saffron. Meadowsweet was also highly regarded as a strewing herb. "The leaves and flowers of meadowsweet," wrote John Gerard in his *Herball or Generall Historie of Plantes* (1597), "farre excelle all other strowing herbs for to decke up houses, to strowe in chambers, halls and banqueting houses in the summer time, for the smell thereof makes the heart merrie and joyful and delighteth the senses." Parkinson (1640) noted that "Queene Elizabeth of famous memorie did more desire meadowsweet than any other sweete herbe to strewe her chambers withall." So fond was Elizabeth of strewn herbs and flowers that she appointed a waiting woman with a fixed salary to always have a ready supply. The office survived until the eighteenth century; in the royal correspondence for 1713 Alice Blizard is cited as "herbe strewer to Her Majesty the Queen."

Yet, royal appointments to the contrary, strewn floors were a rarity in the eighteenth century. As London's burning in 1666 had demonstrated, floors covered with rushes, herbs, and flowers were a great fire hazard; they were also an ideal breeding ground for rats, mice, and fleas. In 1518 a distraught Erasmus wrote to the physician of the cardinal of York: "The floors are strewed with hay and that covered with rushes which are now and then renewed, but not so as to disturb the foundation which sometimes remains for twenty years nursing a collection of spittle, vomit, excrement of dogs and human beings, spilt beer and fish bones and other filth which I need not mention. From this any elevation of temperature, there is exhaled a vapour which in my judgement is by no means beneficial to the human constitution."

Though freshly gathered herbs and flowers would always appeal, the new wealth of the merchant and professional classes, and rising standards of comfort, provoked a desire for decoration of a less fleeting and seasonal kind. Householders who could afford to decorate took as their text the inscription in John Gerard's *Herball*: "to bring all Dame Nature's store into a little room and create a perpetual spring." To this end, walls and ceilings were still painted with garden or landscape-based motifs, but with an extravagance now considered to have been a debasement of ancient practice. At Theobalds, Lord Burghley's country house in Hertfordshire, the main hall was decorated with trees made from natural bark and painted leaves and fruit: "On each side of the hall are six trees having the natural bark so artificially joined with birds nests and leaves as well as fruit upon them, all managed in such a manner that you could not distinguish between the natural and these artificial trees." The illusion deceived even the birds: When the steward opened the window, a German visitor reported in 1592, birds flew in, perched on the trees (in which there were real nests), and began to sing. Queen Elizabeth's chamber at Theobalds was similarly decorated, having "a shew of old oaks and such trees with painted leaves and fruit."

The taste for painted trees was international. In *Hypnerotomachia Poliphili* (1499), Francesco Colonna described how the garden of an Italian palace was continued indoors by means of a long and lofty gallery, "the roof whereof was all painted with a green foliature, with distinct flowers of folded leaves, and little flying birds." A century later painted trees were also the fashion in Germany. In the bedchamber of the landgrave of Hessen, in 1596, a "painted tree . . . grewe up at the doore, the bodie bulking out very naturalie of stone painted bakelike, and the braunches spreading all over the seeling of the chamber full of fruite, and hanging downe upon the walls." Rooms and galleries whose walls and ceilings were covered with painted trunks and branches must have resembled leafy arbors or the "pleached" alleys of gardens in which tree tops were forcibly entwined to provide covered walks.

**EMBROIDERY**

Though wall paintings were popular in the Tudor period, they were rapidly being replaced by hangings. In his *Description of England* (1577), William Harrison referred to "the great amendment of lodging" in his day: "The walls of our houses on the inner sides be either hanged with tapestries, arras work or painted cloths, wherein either divers histories, or herbs, beasts, knots and suchlike are stained, or else they are seeled with oak." Harrison also noted that many small farmers "garnished their beds with tapestry and silk hangings and their tables with carpets and fine napery." One of the oldest means of decorating walls and furniture, not specifically mentioned by Harrison, was to cover them with embroidered cloth. As a means of representing the "herbs, beasts, [and] knots" of the Renaissance garden, embroidery was more effective than Arras work or painted cloths.

The needle was an international instrument, but Englishwomen in particular were renowned for their skill in using it. On his return to Normandy, after Hastings, William astounded his compatriots with the splendor of his embroidered state robes. The Bayeux Tapestry, which technically is an embroidery in colored wools on a ground of coarse linen, is now thought to have been commissioned by the French from an English workshop. Needlework was taught in the medieval convents, and it was also practiced, if not taught, in the monasteries. Thomas Selmiston, a monk who died in 1419, was remembered as an outstanding embroiderer: "For he was in the art of embroidery a most cunning artificier having none like him." In the hierarchy of the arts, needlework ranked with sculpture and manuscript illumination, and it may well have influenced the designs of stained glass windows and book illuminations. Both embroiderers and manuscript illuminators liked filling their surfaces with pattern.

Though associated with religious houses at first, embroidery, like tapestry weaving, became a secular pursuit. By the sixteenth century, except for a guild of professional embroiderers, it was the preserve of gentlewomen and their servants. In castles and manor houses they embroidered altar cloths, church vestments, and hangings for the hall and chapel. Materials were expensive, and the work itself could be done only by women with ample leisure or by servants and retainers who were, in effect, paid to do it. For young women of well-to-do families, proficiency with the needle was regarded as an essential and refined accomplishment. When writing of the school at Wilton Abbey, the seventeenth-century antiquary John Aubrey remarked that "the young mayds were brought up (not as at Hakney, Sarum School, etc. to learn pride and wantonesse) but at the Nunneries where . . . they learnt needlework . . . physik, writing, drawing." In 1693, John Evelyn the diarist wrote of his daughter Susanna on her wedding day: "She is a good child, . . . and qualified with all the ornaments of her sex. She has a peculiar talent in designe . . . and an extraordinary genius for whatever hands can do with a needle."

The chief accomplishments of the women of Elizabeth's court, as listed by Holinshead, were fluency in Latin, Greek, and modern languages and proficiency in spinning, needlework, and music. Women carried their needlework around with them and worked on it both in and out of doors. Embroidery was everywhere. Catherine of Aragon is said to have answered the charges of Henry VIII with a skein of embroidery silk around her neck. A visiting English envoy to the Scottish court described how in council meetings Queen Mary "ordinarily sitteth the most part of the time, sewing at some work or another." Once she was captive, embroidery became her major occupation. "All day she wrought with her Nidyll . . . and continued so long at it till veray Payn made her to give over."

The work of the Elizabethan embroiderers was largely domestic in character and almost entirely secular. Professional embroiderers, who were usually male, were called into the great houses to work on armorial trappings, barge canopies, bed valances, and elaborate costumes for masques and tournaments, but amateur embroiderers—who often were just as skilled—concentrated on dress and informal furnishings for the house.

Despite improvements, northern houses tended to be clammy and cold, and furniture was bulky, cumbersome, and angular. There was also very little of it. Houses were sparsely furnished—beds, a few tables, an occasional cupboard, chairs for the master and mistress, benches and stools for everybody else, and nearly all made of hard, dark oak. Paints, too, tended to be dark, and fire and candlelight cast shadows, so interiors were usually murky. In most rooms fire provided the strongest light, and only rarely would it have been outshone by candles. Thus there was a great need for items that were colorful, warm, and soft. Every conceivable surface became a site for embroidery: pillows, cushions for benches and chairs, table carpets, cupboard carpets, chair covers, window seats, wall hangings, curtains, bedspreads, testers, and valances.

The chief item of furniture was the bedstead. Bedrooms served as studies and parlors as well as sleeping rooms, and the beds could be enormous: 11 feet square in the case of the state beds of Edward vi, Henry vii, and Henry viii. Beds were nearly always in cold and drafty chambers, so sleepers were protected by heavy hangings and valances that, in effect, made a room of the bed. Only the poor slept unprotected: "You know that only the poorest people in England lye without any curtains or vallances," wrote an official of the East India Company in 1683. For those who could afford furnishings, he recommended that the valances be "1 foot deep and 6 yards compass," and the curtains "3 yards wide and 2 yards long."

The valances, which surrounded the bed at the top near the ceiling, were one of the chief fields for the embroiderer's art. They offered large, inviting surfaces that, because they were rigid and seldom touched, were not subject to normal wear and tear. Alone among the bed furnishings they have survived in some quantity. As well as valances and hangings, bedspreads and pillowcases were embroidered. Pillows and cushions were symbols of prosperity and luxury, and they were scattered about the best rooms. In Elizabethan households they were of great importance, reducing the discomfort of oak stools, benches, and window seats. Chairs were covered with cloth or velvet, and this, too, was often embroidered. Walls were usually hung with tapestries, which were woven, but occasionally wall hangings were embroidered.

## SOURCES OF

## EMBROIDERY MOTIFS

*Garden and Hedgerow.* Needlework subjects came overwhelmingly from the garden and the spring and summer landscapes. In scale and complexity they ranged from representations of individual plants and animals, including insects, to entire gardens. In Renaissance embroidery, as in Renaissance painting, gardens and landscapes were settings for incidents taken from the Bible, myth, or allegory, but usually the action was a mere pretext for the display of costume and setting. In a typical arrangement, plants and small animals occupied the immediate foreground, figures and gardens the middle ground and background.

When choosing subjects, needleworkers were guided by previous work and by emblem and pattern books. Women seldom worked directly from nature. Yet their familiarity with the plants and animals of the garden and hedgerow was the mainspring of their art. Gardens and hedgerows were far more prominent in life then than now; and in a world dominated by men, they were generally conceded to be female territory. The male world was the rougher one of field and forest. Food, medicine, and decoration, however, were the housewife's responsibilities, and they gave her undisputed sway over kitchen, herb, and flower garden. John Gerard commended his *Herball* as a work of particular interest to gentlewomen; Thomas Tusser directed his *Five Hundreth Pointes of Good Husbandrie* (1557) at the housewife:

In March and in April from morning to night
In sowing and setting, good housewives delight;
To have in a garden, or other like plot,
To trim up their house, and to furnish their pot.

While men might venture into the kitchen and herb garden, the flower garden was considered the woman's sole domain. John Parkinson described his *Paradisus* (1629), which was frankly devoted to plants distinguished either by their beauty or their fragrance, as a "Feminine [Worke] of Flowers." He dedicated it to Queen Henrietta Maria. His second principal work, *Theatrum Botanicum* (1640), a "Manlike Worke of Herbes and Plants," he dedicated to her husband, Charles i. When John Evelyn visited Lady Clarendon's house at Swallowfield in Berkshire, in 1685, he admired the garden: "My lady being so extraordinarily skilled in the flower, and my lord in diligence of planting."

Flower gardening was conceded to women partly because of a male tendency to associate the fragility and delicacy of flowers with female frailty and partly because flower gardening had lost much of its utility. Flowers were still used for medicines and perfumes, but by the seventeenth century flower gardening would be primarily a diversion particularly suited to leisured well-to-do females. Herbals published early in the seventeenth century listed plants, no longer useful in the still room or the kitchen, which were widely cultivated for the beauty of their flowers.

Men, too, saw gardening as a way of providing sedentary gentlewomen with much-needed exercise: "If the ground be not too much wet," observed a gardener in 1657, "[gentlewomen] may do themselves much good by kneeling upon a cushion and weeding." The cultivation of flowers, like its sister art embroidery, was also seen as an aid to virtue. Gardens, Gerard wrote, "admonish and stir up a man to that which is comely and honest; for floures through their beautie, variety of colour, and exquisite forme, doe bring to a liberal and gentlemanly minde, the remembrance of honestie, comeliness and all kinds of vertues." Refinement and sensibility were associated with flowers of every kind, so that floriculture and gardening were thought to have a civilizing effect on all classes, and both sexes.

As well as improving the morals and pleasing the senses, garden plants were objects of great practical concern. Women had to know how to sow and plant a garden and understand the art of "simpling": the cultivation of herbs and their use in the preparation of medicines. Grace Sherrington, a sixteenth-century housewife, described how she passed her days: "Every day I spent some time in the Herball or books of phisick, and in ministering to one or another by the directions of the best phisitions of myne aquaintance. . . . Also every day I spent some tyme in works of myne owne invention, without sample or patterns before me for carpett or cushion worke, and to drawe flowers and fruit to their lyfe with my pulmmett upon paper."

*Plant Symbolism.* Plants also had symbolic or emblematic significance. The lettered enjoyed a colorful and playful language of allegory rich in veiled meanings. Needleworkers were charmed by the innuendoes of symbolism, and they contrived "conceits," "inventions," and "devices" in much the same way as did Renaissance poets. For instruction and advice they turned to the pictures and verses in emblem books. But there was also a vernacular side to plant symbolism. As emblems of purity, beauty, and the shortness of life, flowers were extensively used in ritual and ceremony. At weddings bridal couples bestowed rosemary (for remembrance) on their friends, and guests carried sprigs of it in their hats. At funerals, evergreens were carried as symbols of immortality. Flowers were sometimes placed on the hearse, and it was customary for children to be buried with them in their hands. The language of flowers, as the historian Keith Thomas observed, had a rich vocabulary, and it was widely spoken. Pansies stood for thoughtfulness, carnations for love, forget-me-nots for remembrance, strawberries

*Young Man amongst the Roses*, Nicholas Hilliard, ca. 1588. Though ostensibly a study in the sadness of unattainable love, there can have been few clearer expressions of the Elizabethan love of flowers and the summer landscape. The white rose, or eglantine, whose leaves and flowers seem embroidered on the young man's cape and hose, was the personal emblem of Elizabeth I. The young man loved his queen. (By courtesy of the Board of Trustees of the Victoria & Albert Museum)

for purity and righteousness, columbines for sadness.

Similar constructions were placed upon the behavior of insects and other animals. Many preachers held that the natural world had been created expressly to teach moral lessons to humans. "God would have a lively image of virtues and vices to be in the creatures," explained the Elizabethan preacher Thomas Wilcox in 1589, "that even in them we might be provoked to virtue and deterred from vice." The thought persisted. George Cheyne, the Hanoverian physician, observed in 1705: "There is scarce beast, bird, reptile nor insect that does not in each particular climate instruct and admonish mankind of some necessary truth for their happiness either in body or mind." Thus moths and flies hinted at the transitoriness of human life, snails at laziness, silk worms at industry, and bees at diligence and orderliness.

In addition to being instructive, insects and other animals were considered beautiful. Elizabethans subscribed to the Platonic and Aristotelean directives that anything that did its work well was beautiful and that natural objects of all kinds should be studied without inhibition or distaste. "If a horse be beautiful in his kind, and a dog in his," asked Thomas Muffett in his *Theater of Insects* (1634), "why should not a beetle be so in its kind? Unless we measure the forms of all things by our own, that what is not like us must be held to be ugly." Like Muffett, Elizabethan embroiderers saw nothing ugly in nature.

*Herbals and Botanical Works.* Needleworkers in search of subjects were able to turn to the world of science as well as that of symbol. The decline of medieval scholasticism, which had been very largely unaffected by experience of the natural world, made possible a revival of the study of botany. Active field naturalists, who laid the foundations of modern botany, zoology, and ornithology, replaced speculative philosophers. Illustrated herbals, botanies, and books on gardening were, thanks to the invention of printing, distributed widely, and embroiderers, who were hungry for models, fell upon them. Even Thomas Tusser's *Five Hundreth Pointes of Good Husbandrie* (1557), which had very little material on flowers, became (according to the historian of needlework, Lanto Synge) part of the grammar of embroidery. Swiss naturalist Conrad Gesner's *Catalogus Plantarum* (1542) and *Historia Animalium* (1551) were available in England and must have provided useful material for embroiderers. England's first printed herbal, John Gerard's *Herball* (1597), was as popular with needleworkers as with apothecaries. John Parkinson's *Paradisus* (1629), the first English herbal to devote itself to ornamental flowers, was also immensely popular with embroiderers.

Other books, masquerading as natural histories, were aimed directly at the needleworker. Thomas Johnson's *Book of Beasts, Birds, Flowers, Fruits, Flies and Wormes, exactly drawne with their Lively Colors truly Described* (1630) consisted of engravings borrowed from Dutch, English, and German sources and printed in unrelated scales. In 1650 Peter Stent published a *Booke of Flowers Fruits Beastes Birds and Flies* and, as a convenience to needleworkers and others, offered engravings in sheet form. Pattern books for embroiderers, which were available after 1550, offered very similar fare. Richard Shoreleyker's *Schole House for the Needle* (1624) contained "sundry sorts of spots as Flowers, Birds, Fishes, etc," designed to be wrought at the needleworker's pleasure—"some with Gould, some with Silke, and some with Crewell."

The simple, clean-edged woodcuts used to illustrate the first printed botanical works were particularly easy for needleworkers and pattern makers to copy. Designed for physicians and apothecaries, the illustrations in the herbals had one purpose only: to facilitate identification of the plants. In the preface to his distinguished herbal *De Historia Sturpium* (1542), Leonhart Fuchs was careful to explain that everything possible had been done to ensure the clarity of the figures. The drawings were made from living plants, and by keeping his team of artists and engravers on a tight rein, he was able to eliminate "shadows, and other less necessary things" that tended to glorify the artist, not the plant.

Metal engraving, which produces a finer line than wood engraving, allowed greater attention to detail, but in the interests of highlighting the identifying features of the plants, many metal engravers retained the bold, graceful outlines that embroiderers found both useful and attractive. Tendencies toward clarity in illustration were also reinforced by changes in the nature of botany itself. From being "one of the handmaids of physick" (so described by William Coles in 1656) botany, by the late eighteenth century, had developed an identity of its own. Plants were being studied for their own sake, not just for their usefulness to humans. Increasingly, therefore, European botanists were inclined to group plants according to their intrinsic structural characteristics, not their usefulness to human beings. Most classifications thus concentrated on external visible features such as the character of the leaves, the fruit, and the flower.

The printing press, and the popularity of gardening and floriculture, also led to a rapid increase in the number of gardening books. If illustrated, these, too, were pored over by needleworkers. In the sixteenth century there were only about nineteen new titles on botany and horticulture, in the seventeenth about a hundred, and in the eighteenth no fewer than six hundred. The increase reflected an expansion of interest in flowers on a scale so great as to warrant its being dubbed a "gardening revolution." To some extent this

# Renaissance House and Garden

revolution was an English phenomenon. It hardly touched Wales and Scotland, and it was much less advanced on the Continent. In 1705 one nursery in London alone, Brompton Park, probably contained as many plants—nearly ten million—as all the nurseries of France.

*Strange and Outlandish Plants.* A great stimulant to ornamental gardening, and to embroidery, was the influx of exotic flowers and shrubs, Maeterlinck's "invasion of sunlight," which followed the reestablishment of trade with the Levant and the voyages of exploration and discovery. England also benefited from Flemish refugees, threatened by Spanish persecution, who brought with them flowers recently introduced to the Low Countries from Asia Minor. "It is a world also to see how many strange herbs, plants and annual fruits are daily brought to us from the Indies, Americas, Taprobane, Canary Islands and all parts of the world," wrote William Harrison in 1577. Harrison also commented on how quickly they were assimilated into English gardens: "There is not almost one noble gentleman or merchant that hath not great store of these flowers, which now also begin to wax so well acquainted with our soils that we may almost account of them as parcel of our own commodities." Many of the introductions were commercial and industrial plants (hops, saffron, woad, flax, hemp, and madder) or fruit and vegetables (potatoes, red peppers, and artichokes), but most were acquired for curiosity and display. Even the runner bean was first introduced for the sake of its flowers.

In *Paradisus* John Parkinson distinguished between England's "owne bred flowers," such as pansies, and "strange and outlandish" ones such as anemones, tulips, Michaelmas daisies, the yellow crocus, evening primrose, and nasturtium. His age, he averred, had "more delighted in the search, curiosity and rarities of these delights than any age . . . before." Some of the new plants were so fragrant and so richly blossomed that a few of them could perfume and decorate a whole chamber. But in general it was the appearance of the exotics which excited interest, and it led to the cultivation of flowers exclusively for their visual qualities. Garden design took a new direction as a result; it became an art of arrangement and ultimately of views and perspectives. The exotics also extended the flowering season. By showing forth the beauty and bravery of their colors so early in the year, Parkinson remarked, "they seeme to make a Garden of Delight even in the Winter time."

Pattern engravers soon began to avail themselves of the treasures of botanists and naturalists. Plants, flowers, and insects and others animals (the last two principally from Conrad Gesner's *Historia Animalium*) were painted in watercolor and used as models for woodcuts and engravings to illustrate botanical works and herbals. Botanical drawing had begun as a practical art to enable herbalists to identify the plants they used for their medicines. But with time there was an increased tendency to draw or paint flowers, not for use, as in the herbals, but simply for their beauty. In households that could afford a few books, botanical works were mined for illustrations that might serve as models for embroideries. Delight in the new species was expressed in descriptions of colors so delicate and exact that we hardly recognize them today: Tulips, for example, could combine tones of gredeline (pale gray), quoist (the color of a dove's breast), and gilvus (a very pale red). By 1620 flower patterns were beginning to dominate the minor arts, and following the "tulipomania" of the 1630s they would be triumphant. Lace makers, embroiderers, tapestry weavers, goldsmiths, woodcarvers, and printers all found in flowers the subjects they needed.

The first overseas plant to stir the European fancy was the anemone, or "windflower," and the enthusiasm for it was a portent of the reception awaiting the tulip. The first tulip bulbs were brought from Istanbul to Vienna in 1554, and from there they were taken to France, Holland, and England, whose shores, according to Richard Hakluyt, they reached before 1582. Both Parkinson and Gerard fell before the tulip's beauty. Parkinson considered the flower "above and beyond all others"; Gerard opined: "Nature [seemed] to play more with this floure than with any other that I do know." Besides a glorious variety of color, tulips carry, Parkinson noted, "so stately and delightfull a forme, and do abide so long in their bravery (enduring above three whole months from the first unto the last) that there is no Lady or Gentlewoman of any worth that is not caught with this delight or not delighted with these flowers."

The tulip was one of the first plants to be admired for its appearance alone. Lacking both fragrance and "vertue" (medicinal or culinary properties), it was, to adapt Maeterlinck's phrase, a dazzling but chilly kinswoman from abroad. Thomas Fuller, in his *Antheologia, or The Speech of Flowers*, made the point much earlier (1642) by inventing a complaint from an indignant rose: Despite its scent and the healing cordials that could be made from its syrups, since the advent of the tulip it had been "neglected and contemned." The "toolip," by contrast, was no more than a "well complexioned stink—an ill savour wrapt up in pleasant colors" which was so useless to medicine that no physician had honored it with a Latin name. Once they were admired for their appearance alone, flowers became as vulnerable to fashion as clothes.

In addition to the movement of plants from country to country, there was also a movement of botanical illustrators. Good illustrators were much sought after. England, which was not blessed with talented flower painters, became an eager patron of painters from the Continent. But not all movements were voluntary. The brilliant Huguenot illustrator Jacques Le Moyne de Morgues came to England in 1572, following the St. Bartholomew's Day massacre. In 1586 he published *La clef des champs*, a book of ninety-eight simple, uncluttered woodcuts based on his watercolors of flowers, fruits, and animals. Le Moyne's dedication explained that the book was designed to serve the interests of noble patrons and those artisans—goldsmiths, embroiderers, and tapestry makers—who depended on the work of painters. If proof were needed of its value to needleworkers, the telltale pricking of the copies in the British Museum speaks eloquently of an embroiderer's impatience to use the motifs. In the absence of a traveling draftsman selling ready-made patterns, an embroiderer would prick the outlines of book illustrations and then dust or pounce charcoal through the holes to transfer the design onto the piece of stuff to be worked.

Embroiderers and designers in the capitals and large cities also had access to botanical gardens created especially for the cultivation of exotic plants. Pierre Vallet, embroiderer to Henry IV (reigned 1589–1610) of France, based many of his designs on the gardens of the Louvre, which were filled with plants from all corners of the known world. The gardens were the creation of Jean Robin, who had set out to meet the demand for rare, and often delicate, plants by opening a garden equipped with hothouses. So successful was Robin that within a few years Henry IV had bought the garden, known subsequently as the Jardin du Roi or Jardin des Plantes. In 1608 Pierre Vallet, using sketches from the garden, published *Le Jardin du Roi très Chrestien Henry IV* (1608), a pattern book for embroiderers. It was the first book devoted exclusively to ornamental plants, that is, to plants that "are worthy of note only because of the elegance of their flowers."

**EMBROIDERY'S**

**AFFINITIES WITH**

**GARDENING**

The needle is a versatile instrument, and in skilled hands there were few subjects it could not be made to reproduce. Equipped with fine colored silks and the new steel needle, which replaced the drawn-wire one, Renaissance embroiderers were marvels of inventiveness. James Boler opened his book *The Needle's Excellency* (1634) with an ode (written by John Taylor) to their versatility:

Flowers, plants and fishes, beasts, birds, flyes, and bees,
Hills, dales, plaines, pastures, skies, seas, rivers, trees;
There's nothing neere at hand, or farthest sought,
But with the needle may be shaped and wrought.

**Ladies working at their embroidery in a pleasure garden, from the Album of Gervasius Fabricius of Salzburg, 1613. Embroiderers seldom worked directly from nature, but their familiarity with plants, along with the significance they accorded them, was the chief source of their art. The garden retains the carpenter's work, geometrical knots, and fountain of an earlier age. (By permission of the British Library)**

Though embroiderers could represent hills, dales, rivers, and trees, embroidery's true affinity was with the garden. The didactic title page of Boler's book, in fact, shows an embroiderer, representing the virtue Industry, sitting in a garden of small square beds surrounded by a trellis fence interwoven with flowers. Like most sixteenth- and seventeenth-century embroiderers, she would have been trying to record the appearance of the garden at its peak. Her subjects would have ranged from the entire garden to the smallest flowers and insects within it. Miniature garden scenes illustrated every detail of the layouts except—because of the smallness of the scale—the actual plants in the beds.

Individual plants and insects were shown in detail on cushions and cur-

# Renaissance House and Garden

tains and on clothing. Functional articles of clothing, heavily embroidered, were a mark of high station. Embroidered gloves, for example, set their owners apart from manual laborers, who, in the days before the antiseptic treatment of infections, wore plain, unpatterned gloves to protect their hands. Embroidered costume was particularly fashionable in England. Philip Stubbes wrote in 1583 that fashionable hose must be "wrought all over, from the gartering upward, with needlework clogged with silk of all colours, with birds, foules, beasts, and antiques." And in Lord North's household book (1581) there is an entry for "Froggs and Flies for the Queen's gloves." The fashion for embroidered costumes peaked between the middle of the sixteenth century and the Civil War, but it was popular at least as early as the fourteenth century. Readers of the *Canterbury Tales* may remember Chaucer's squire: "Embroidered was he, as it were a mede / Al ful of freshe floures whyte and rede."

Embroidery and gardening were quickly seen to be sister, or complementary, arts. Each required application and attention to detail. In the Renaissance garden, as on the embroiderer's ground, each plant had to be tended individually and, in matters of grafting, pruning, and transplanting, painstakingly. There were also distinct physical similarities between the products of the two arts. Both depended heavily on pattern for their effects; the only known English designer of knot gardens, Thomas Trevelyan, also designed patterns for embroideries. Needlework on a linen or canvas ground not only resembles ground-hugging plants, but its texture (as Thomasina Beck pointed out in 1979) also has qualities of depth, softness, and warmth which even the most subtle painting cannot match. When Sir Thomas Platter visited the Palace of Nonsuch in 1599, he found the embroideries to be so lifelike that the flowers and shrubs seem to have been planted, "to be growing indeed." Outside, in the gardens, he reversed the coin: The plants were mingled in such intricate circles that they might have been drawn by the needle of Semiramis.

So compatible were gardening and embroidery that practitioners and observers began to think of one in terms of the other. In the dedication of his *Herball* (1597), John Gerard took embroidery as his metaphor: "What greater delight is there than to behold the earth apparelled with plants, as with a robe of imbroidered works, set with orient pearles and garnished with great diversitie of rare and costly jewels." Both gardeners and embroiderers liked to mix their plants, posy-fashion:

> Emerald tufts, flowers, purple, blue and white,
> Like sapphires, pearls and rich embroidery.
> (Shakespeare, *The Merry Wives of Windsor*)

When advising gardeners on how tulips should be planted, John Parkinson intimated that the practice of mixing plants of different colors had been initiated by the needleworker: "one color answering and setting off another that the place where they stand may resemble a peece of curious needlework." In 1669 John Worlidge spoke of an elder tree whose leaves seemed to be "embroidered" by the swelling of the veins. The association between gardening and needlework persisted down to modern times: William Morris urged embroiderers to think of their work as "gardening with silk and thread." Inevitably, the vocabulary of needlework entered gardening; the rows in which flowers were planted were sometimes described as threads, and the curved lines of the flowers as ribbons; planted beds could be embroidered or brocaded, and French gardeners created parterres of embroidery.

Renaissance gardeners and needleworkers liked nothing better than to cover the surface of their respective grounds with intense, intricate patterns: with "knots so enknotted it cannot be express't." The ideal garden, like the ideal embroidery, was a place where, as Thomas Campion put it in 1601, all was work and nowhere space:

> And would you see my mistress' face
> It is a flowery garden place
> Where knots of beauties have such grace
> That all is work and nowhere space.

Particularly dense were the intricate coiling patterns of "blackwork," the name given to embroidery in one color—usually black, though sometimes red. As if to celebrate their ingenuity, "blackworkers," in imitation of arbors made of tightly interwoven plants, liked to show many different blossoms apparently growing from a single stem. "You shall set white thorne, eglantine and sweet briar mixt together," wrote Gervase Markham early in the seventeenth century, "and they shall shoot and grow up so shall you wind and pleach them within the lattice work making them grow and cover the same." The trailing coils of blackwork might well have been in Christopher Marlowe's mind when he compared honeysuckle and rose stems interwoven above a stream to a piece of embroidery: "and as a costly valance o'er a bed, So did their garland tops the brook o'er spread." Blackwork, too, was the ideal medium for representing "closed knots," that is, knots so tight that there was no room for flowers.

In gardening, as in decoration, the Renaissance objective was to improve nature or "correct" it: "t'excell the natural with made delights," as Edmund Spenser put it in 1579. To achieve this, gardeners made tightly organized gardens with, to quote Spenser again, "every herbe there set in order." Wherever possible, too, they gilded the lily by making the decorative qualities of plants even more brilliant. The ultimate expression of this was the practice of "candying" living herbs and flowers. On hot summer mornings, as soon as the dew was dry, Elizabethans would moisten petals of balm, sage, or borage with a mixture of gum and rose water, sprinkle them with fine sugar, and then let them dry. Candied petals or blooms could be eaten, but the main object of the exercise was to extend the bloom of youth, if only for a few hours. As Sir Hugh Platt (*Floraes Paradise*) noted, it enabled the blooms to remain "a long time notwithstanding the violence of the rain."

In similar ways, embroiderers exaggerated the decorative qualities of plants by using gold or silver threads and even pearls and jewels. Elaborately embroidered costumes and decorative gardens were perfect complements for each other. During open-air entertainments, silk, satin, and velvet costumes embroidered with a dazzling array of small flowers, leaves, birds, and insects worked in bright silks and brilliant metal threads must have glittered as alluringly as the gilded and crystallized confections growing around them.

Nothing reflected the Renaissance interest in the exotic and the strange more clearly than the enthusiasm for raised work, or stumpwork. To represent the outlandish plants and topiary of gardens that had become ever more elaborate, embroiderers in the second half of the seventeenth century resorted to a third dimension when making picture panels, mirror frames, and covers for chests and cabinets. Material was stuffed with small blocks of wood, cotton wool, or hair to create relief and then embroidered on the stamp, or stump. In this way figures were elevated "above the grounding." Ingenious needlewomen, too, were able to make flower petals, and even entire plants, lift off the surface of the material. Completely detached motifs, which were cut out and applied to another surface, were known as "slips," the gardener's word for a cutting taken from a plant for grafting or planting. By concealing fine wire and padding in the stitchery of raised work, fruit and snail shells were made to swell realistically. Even more elaborate shapes could be rendered by working flowers and other subjects within flexible wire frames. The practice was in direct imitation of topiary, the gardener's method of training yew and rosemary around wire frames to assume the shapes of dogs, fowl, and fish.

But the mania for what the English poet and writer Edmund Gosse called splendid impossibilities went beyond topiary. Mesmerized by the beauty and fragrance of outlandish flowers, gardeners attempted to change both the appearance and the scent of plants. In experiments that Parkinson in 1640 dismissed as "beyond both reason and nature," gardeners made slits in the bark of trees and soaked them in musk or cinnamon so that the leaves of the trees might bud out scented. Others believed that white lilies could be

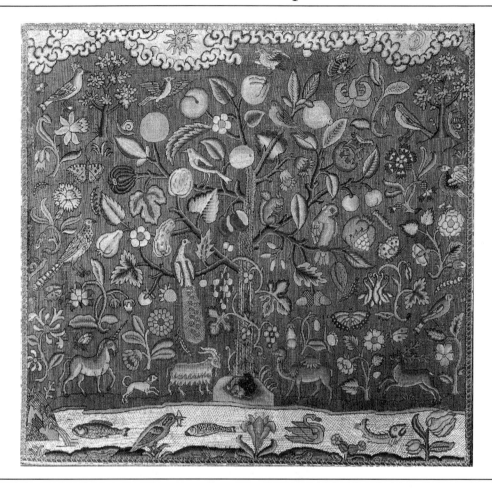

**Fruiting tree embroidered in silks, seventeenth century. In experiments that went "beyond reason and nature," seventeenth-century gardeners tried to change the form, the fruit, and the scent of plants. Embroiderers sometimes succeeded where gardeners and horticulturists usually failed. (All rights reserved, The Metropolitan Museum of Art. Gift of Irwin Untermyer, 1964 [64.101.1305])**

turned into scarlet ones by rubbing cinnabar between the rind and the small buds growing about the root; that a white damask rose could be grafted on a stalk of broom to get yellow roses; that verdigris poured into the opened top of a tulip bulb would produce a green blossom. What gardeners failed to achieve in fact, embroiderers and stumpworkers realized to some degree in fancy through the bizarre plants and trees and unnaturally bright flowers that they applied to cabinets, trunks, and the frames of mirrors.

For ingenious embroiderers, pools, fountains, and—those oddities of the seventeenth-century garden—grottoes also provided opportunities for virtuoso performances that called upon every stitch and material at the embroiderer's command. Water was patterned horizontally and rocks verti-

# Renaissance House and Garden

cally, and tiny spirals of purl (coils of silk-covered wire) along with beads and spangles simulated the glinting minerals on the walls of actual grottoes. Fish ponds were also a challenge. The gleaming bodies of the fish as they turned or leapt in the sun, and the bright plumage of the birds that swam among them, tested the embroiderer's talents. The brilliant creations or embellishments of the embroiderers encouraged gardeners and landscape designers to exceed the natural with even greater delights. At Hatfield House artificial fish were set among carefully laid rocks and colored shells in a stream bed and were animated by water poured onto them from a marble basin. The basin, dominated by a statue of Neptune, stood on painted artificial rocks. On Francis Bacon's estate at Gorhambury there were, presumably, no knots, but Sir Francis had his own toys. Around the shore of the lake were gilt images and "glasses coloured for the eye"; the bottom of the lake was covered with pebbles of several colors worked into the shapes of fish and other figures.

Though products of very active fancies, "riotous excesse[s]" of this sort were the final expressions of an old tendency, not the beginnings of a new one. Gardens in general were becoming less, not more, decorative: "Walked to Whitehall . . . discoursing of the present fashion of gardens to make them plain," read Pepys' diary entry for July 22, 1666. Pepys' walk had probably taken him past, or through, St. James's Park, the first park in England to be laid out along French lines. Charles II (reigned 1660–85) had called in French gardeners to design the park, and so great was their influence that in fashionable gardens throughout England simple grass plots replaced the medley of plants in the knots. In the new gardens there was more space than work. The knot and its associated beds of flowers gave way to *broderies par terre*, in which box or turf was laid out in scrolling lines to imitate some of the simpler kinds of embroidery. André Mollet (1670) pointed out that for the smaller, "neater embroidery," box, and particularly dwarf box, was usually preferred because it could be planted and clipped to produce any shape and required less attention than turf. Because of its strong and, for some people, unpleasant smell, box was particularly suitable for "ground embroidery."

As gardening became more formal and architectural, the decorative value of the flower declined. A simple parterre might have a border of flowers, but the ground between the scrolling lines of box and grasswork was usually covered with sand, brick dust, or gravel; the classical mind took pleasure in form and design, not variety of color. By the end of the seventeenth century entirely flowerless beds were being laid out, not because the love of flowers had been lost, but because their irregular growth would have smudged the clear lines of the design. Even in England, where the love of flowers was unparalleled, plain turf plots showing off the excellence of English grass replaced flowery beds in many a garden. Pepys, a convert to the new style, suggested that flowers should be grown in a "little plot by themselves" out of sight of the main garden and that they should be of the sort that grow "very low lest they spoil the beauty of the embroidery." His opinion was shared by Sir Thomas Hanmer. In his *Garden Book* (1659) he banished flowers to the remote parts of the garden, allowing near the house only those "such as grow very low."

Not all gardeners were enamored of the French style, and resistance to it was probably strongest in England. In 1665 the naturalist John Rea dismissed French formalism as an "immured nothing," preferring the "essential ornaments, the verdant carpets of many pretty plants and pleasing flowers" with which even a green meadow was "spontaneously embroidered." John Worlidge in 1669 complained that gravel walks and grass plots, the new "Presidents" of many stately country residences, had "banished out of their Gardens, Flowers, the Miracles of Nature and best Ornaments that ever were discovered to make a Seat pleasant." The affection for flowers persisted even in the inner sanctum of French formalism, the Palace of Versailles itself. In 1663 the king's rooms were filled with jasmine, his favorite flower. Yet despite the resistance to flowerless formality, sophisticated interest was turning away from circumscribed flower and botanical gardens to the avenues and sweeping parterres of the gardens of Le Notre. Progressive gardeners were looking beyond the knot garden and the lattice fence with a view to merging garden and countryside.

As perspectives broadened, people turned away from the particularities of nature. Samuel Johnson declared that "man should not number the streaks of the tulip or describe the different shapes of the verdure of the forest" but must generalize, "neglecting minuter discriminations." Women, who were less hampered by classical education, still saw nature in detail, so the practice of floral embroidery continued. In eighteenth-century Scotland, for example, the expression "the Flooerin'" was instantly recognizable as the practice of embroidering flowers on white cotton. But the period when embroidery could dominate interior decoration had ended, and it would never again achieve the brilliance of its blissful marriage to knot gardening. Embroidered parterres to the contrary, embroiderers throve on "minuter discriminations," on the near view and small-scale picturesque vignettes. The sweeping spaces of the formal French garden and the even broader prospects of the English landscaped estate were not beyond the scope of the domestic embroiderer, but they lay outside her natural province, and for the most part she left the representation of them to painters and tapestry weavers.

# Outlandish Landscapes

ad Thomas Fuller, the seventeenth-century defender of the English rose, been concerned with interiors as well as gardens, he would have been exercised to see outlandish plants, and the environments in which they grew, vying with native ones as motifs in decoration. Reports from voyagers returned from distant lands, and an influx of goods from the Near East, India, and China as trade routes opened, excited European imaginations. Addison wrote an essay on the glories of overseas commerce, and Pope celebrated them in a couplet: "This casket India's glowing gems unlocks, / And all Arabia breathes from yonder box." Foreign plants, gardens, and landscapes—or in some cases, European conceptions of them—became as acceptable as native ones. They were to play an increasingly important role in decoration.

**PERSIAN GARDENS AND CARPETS**

Oriental carpets, with garden motifs, were the first invaders. An astonished Matthew Paris related that when Eleanor of Castile came to England to marry Edward I in 1254, her ambassadors covered the very floors of her lodgings with carpets from Spain and the Orient. And when she arrived at Westminster, she found her apartments furnished with costly hangings and "like a church carpeted," after the Spanish fashion. The English fashion in the thirteenth century was to cover floors with rushes and herbs. By the sixteenth century rushes were generally woven into matting rather than scattered loose, but in 1598 an indignant foreign visitor could still describe one of Queen Elizabeth's presence chambers as "strewed with hay."

But the intransigence of the royal household was not characteristic of England as a whole; rush matting was in general use, and woven and knotted carpets from Persia and Turkey, then used as table rather than floor covers, were common enough to be almost standard props in paintings of fashionable interiors. Cardinal Wolsey's private accounts, however, record the purchase of "foot carpets," and even Queen Elizabeth owned a Turkish carpet that she sometimes placed on the floor instead of rushes.

Virtually all Oriental carpets expressed in some form or other the spirit of the garden. On the Iranian plateau, the source of the most prized carpets, gardens were refuges from a difficult climate and, as Richard Ettinghausen pointed out in 1967, an unprepossessing landscape: "immense, barren, monotonously brown or grey vistas, glaringly hot or windswept . . . [and] equally monotonous earth-colored towns or villages haphazardly built up without planning or loving care." Understandably, Persian rulers and the rich spent much of their time in gardens, and even when traveling they rested en route in gardens created for the purpose. Xenophon noted (in *Oeconomicus*) that "in whatever countries the [Persian] king resides, or wherever he travels, he is concerned that there be gardens, the so-called pleasure gardens, filled with all the fine and good things that the earth wishes to bring forth, and in these he himself spends most of his time, when the season of the year doesn't preclude it." For Persians, as for most people in the Near East, bliss was a garden that never lacked blossoms, fragrant herbs, lush grasses, and cool water.

The classic Persian garden was a rectangular plot divided into four equal parts by two paths intersecting at right angles. A shallow pool often marked the central intersection, and in larger gardens the paths were flanked by canals. Diagonals were possible within the rectangular scheme, but the basic plan was always cross-shaped—an expression, so it is believed, of the ancient cosmological ideal of a quartered universe which found its first literary expression in the second chapter of Genesis: "And a river went out of Eden to water the garden; and from thence it was parted, and became into four heads." A quadrangular design also served the needs of irrigation, straight canals being the most effective.

For privacy, and for protection against wind, sand, and dust, Persian gardens were enclosed by high brick walls. Within them grew shade trees, fruit

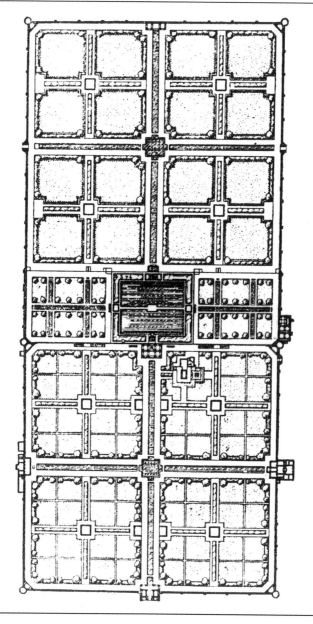

**Plan of a Persian garden. The classic type was a rectangular plot divided into four equal parts by two paths intersecting at right angles. A shallow pool often marked the central intersection.**

trees, and flowers—particular favorites were roses and narcissi for their beauty and jasmine for its sweet scent. Trees, too, were coveted; the planting and care of them is said to have been an important part of Persians' education, and a mystical feeling for them part of their tradition. Persians were as fond of tree houses as were Europeans. In larger gardens, swans were com-

Persian miniature, 1430–40. Paradise was a walled garden — with flowering trees, flower-spangled turf, and a life-giving stream. (Musée des Arts Décoratifs, Paris; all rights reserved)

# Outlandish Landscapes

mon on water courses, and there were also ducks, deer, and pheasants; smaller birds were housed in aviaries. The aviary in the garden of the Chahil Sutun delighted the English diplomat Sir Thomas Herbert: "And the garden or wilderness behind the house was made fragrant with flowers, filled with airy citizens privileged from hurt or affrights, and for which they return their thankful notes in a more melodious concert and variety than if they were in the exactest vollyere (aviary) in the universe" (1677).

During the hot summers Persians retreated to their gardens for several days at a time, and in them, unlike the more active Europeans in their gardens, they sat and absorbed the light, colors, and smells. A Persian garden, remarked the seventeenth-century traveler Sir John Chardin, was a place to occupy rather than walk through: "The Persians don't walk so much in gardens as we do, but content themselves with a bare Prospect, and breathing the fresh Air: for this End, they set themselves down in some part of the Garden, at their first coming into it, and never move from their Seats till they are going out of it." A connoisseurial attitude to gardens spread throughout the Islamic world. The beauty of changing light in a garden gave such pleasure that a man from Mosul (in Iraq) thought it worth traveling to Cairo just to see the evening shadows move obliquely across its gardens. Persian and Islamic feelings for gardens went into their naming: Heart Delighting Garden, Garden of Purity, Garden of Fidelity, Sojourn of Felicity.

For Persians, gardens were so important that in winter, when their surroundings were more colorless and cold than usual, they had to contrive substitutes for them. "He who cannot traverse mountains and lakes," went a Chinese saying popular in Persia, "will find great joy in a landscape born of a skilled hand." Persian kings set over their thrones and couches fruiting trees and vines made from gold and precious stones. Courtiers and commoners, who had to find less extravagant solutions, bought colorful miniature gardens made from paper, paste, paint, and wax by artisans known as "date palm setters." The practice persisted into the early modern period: In 1759 Cornelius le Brun reported, "On the tenth [of February] it is customary for the courtiers to make their voluntary presents to his majesty, consisting principally of wax-works, artfully wrought up in the form of houses, gardens, fine flowers, or fruits."

Though popular, the miniature artificial garden was not the most satisfying garden substitute. Far more evocative was a carpet laid out like a garden. The classic carpet design had a central tank from which four channels led to a peripheral canal. The border of the carpet was called *su*, the Arabic word for water, and the Arabic word for earth was used for the foundation or ground. The carpets were decorated with representations of cypress and

The spirit of the garden: the *Wagner Garden Carpet*, Persian, seventeenth century. The carpet is of traditional design, with central pool, water channels, pathways, trees, flowers, birds, fish, and other animals. (Burrell Collection, Glasgow Museums and Art Galleries, with permission)

plane trees, flowers such as peonies, water lilies, and irises, and the large birds of the garden: herons, pelicans, and ducks. Verses set in panels on the borders of some of the carpets spoke of flowers, raindrops, wind, and dew and of the ineffable desire, in a cold desert, for perpetual spring.

As well as being surrogates for spring and summer landscapes, carpets, like tapestries and embroideries, were functional. Winters in Persia were cold and methods of house construction often primitive. Floors were usually made of mud, laid over poplar poles and branches, and without some form of covering the dust would have been intolerable, and the floor would quickly have worn away. Mud floors were also extremely hard. In *Cyropaedia*, his book on the beginnings of the Persian Empire, Xenophon noted that carpets were spread under couches "so that the floor should not offer hard resistance."

The finest carpets were spread only on ceremonial occasions, and sometimes they were hung on walls rather than laid on floors. Fine carpets were held in such esteem that Shah Abbas I, according to a seventeenth-century French traveler, would not step on one until servants had removed his shoes. Display carpets, which must often have been laid out in scented rooms, had the greatest power to suggest the garden. A fine garden carpet, noted a twentieth-century Iranian weaver, is a dream of permanence: "Here in the fresh garden blooms an ever lovely spring, unhurt by Autumn gales or winter storms." Richard Ettinghausen, a twentieth-century professor, made a similar point: "The Safavid carpet had functions of a psychological nature beyond its basic service as a warm, soft and handsome floor covering. . . . Better than a garden, these carpets are *in* the house and exist in all seasons." For people sitting on or near the carpets their "studied order," Ettinghausen added, "with all [its] intricacy, was undoubtedly just as deeply satisfying as . . . the formalism of the Persian garden."

According to one sixteenth-century source, carpets were brought from storage during the cold season and banquets held on them, just as in summer they were held in actual gardens. Persian poets, too, exalted the garden carpet's power of suggestion. The lines of verse that follow were woven into the border of a sixteenth-century carpet: "This is not a carpet, it is a white rose . . . No, it is more, it is a garden filled with lilies and roses; its beauty draws the nightingales here to sing. Look at the cascades of water that spring from its weave on every side, this is the way to the spring of youth . . . Nowhere is there a single flaw in this perfect grace . . . Oh God, this pure rose is the flawless child in the garden of hope."

The most famous of all Persian carpets, woven during the reign of Chosroes I (531–79), represented the flowers, trees, and streams of a springtime garden. Flower beds were fashioned from colored gemstones, and streams, canals, and pools from bright, clear crystals, roughly the size of pearls. The ground of the carpet was worked in gold to look yellow, like earth. Tree trunks and branches were made of gold or silver; leaves were of silk, and blossoms of colored gemstones. An outer border of solid emeralds represented a meadow or a grassy field. Made for the audience hall of the palace at Ctesiphon, the capital of the Sassanid kings, the carpet reputedly was 80 feet wide and 200 feet long. The Arab conquerors of the Sassanids are said to have been overwhelmed by its magnificence, but admiration did not prevent them from cutting it into strips and selling the pieces to jewelers.

Two other kinds of carpets, flower carpets and hunting and animal carpets, also expressed Persian affection for gardens and parks. The flower carpet was a variation of the garden carpet: Masses of flowers, trees, and interconnecting vines, frequently grouped around a tree of life or a central medallion of patterned flowers and stems, completely covered the ground. Just as flower and garden carpets re-created the delights of the Persian garden, so animal and hunting carpets rekindled the excitement of the chase. Game was pursued either in great walled hunting parks or in sealed valleys into which the animals had been driven. In the hunting carpets, riders armed with lances and bows pursue lions, jackals, foxes, antelopes, ibexes, wild boars, and hares. Tigers and panthers romp or charge amid blossoms of lotus and peony or lie in the shade of cypress, pomegranate, almond, and magnolia trees.

In Europe, carpets were widely used as wall hangings and as coverings for tables and floors. Crusaders returning from the Holy Land in the eleventh century introduced the Oriental carpet to transalpine Europe, but as an item of trade it was first brought in by Italian merchants with connections in the Levant. Anatolia in central Turkey was a major producer of carpets, and since virtually all Oriental wares bound for Western markets passed through Istanbul, the name Turkey became the generic word for an Oriental carpet regardless of its place of origin; thus a carpet made in Persia could be described as a *tapis de Turquie persan*.

Both Persian and Turkish carpets were immediately popular, and in the fourteenth and fifteenth centuries wealthy citizens of Venice, Genoa, and Florence might have owned as many as ten to fifteen of them. "There could be no house of quality," noted Leonardo da Vinci, "which was not furnished with Turkish materials and rugs." A measure of the popularity of these carpets is the frequency with which they occur in Italian paintings. They appeared first in the paintings of Simone Martini, at the beginning of the fourteenth century, and in paintings by Ghirlandaio, Carpaccio, Lorenzo de Credi, and Lorenzo Lotto in the fifteenth and sixteenth centuries. In Italy, a Lotto described a carpet as well as a painting.

Oriental carpets were equally popular north of the Alps; from the four-

Tree and garden carpet, Persian, early sixteenth century. Flowers and trees completely cover the ground, as in a verdure or millefleurs tapestry. Carpets so rich in detail were meant to be looked at carefully; Persian rooms were sparsely furnished, and people sat either on the floor or on cushions or low divans. (Philadelphia Museum of Art: The Joseph Lees Williams Memorial Collection)

teenth century, Jewish and Armenian merchants had permanent trading posts in Bruges. An inventory made for the duc de Berry (1340–1416), who was an indefatigable collector, listed "two carpets . . . with green foliage, made in Turkey." Cardinal Wolsey, Henry VIII's powerful Lord Chancellor, furnished Hampton Court with sixty carpets that he acquired from Venice through the offices of the Venetian ambassador in London. Wolsey's purchase started a fashion. Oriental carpets appear so frequently in the portraits of Hans Holbein the Younger (1497–1543) that the paintings are now used as an index to the carpets of the period.

Happily for Europe, the popularity of Oriental carpets coincided with a particularly productive period in the history of Persian carpet making. Release from years of Seljuk and Mongol domination, early in the sixteenth century, triggered a renaissance of the arts which was guided by the enlightened Shah Abbas I. The shah built workshops and factories and opened schools for designers. Production increased rapidly, and because of the accessibility of the eastern Mediterranean and the large size of the European merchant fleets, shipments of carpets moved steadily from east to west. The sixteenth century also saw a relaxation of Islamic sanctions, which in Persia seem never to have been strong, against the naturalistic representation of plants and animals. By using fine silk thread in the pile of the carpet, as well as in the warp and the weft, Persian weavers were able to render details so precisely that their garden and hunting carpets, so their admirers claim, were nothing less than knotted illuminations.

When Henry VIII divorced Catherine of Aragon in 1529, England forfeited its access to Mediterranean sources of Oriental carpets. Spain and the other Catholic countries closed Mediterranean ports to British shipping, and they were not reopened until Drake's defeat of the Spanish Armada in 1588. Encouraged by Cardinal Wolsey, the English, who had an abundance of wool, began to weave their own carpets. For motifs, weavers, like needleworkers, looked to the English garden; sixteenth-century hand-knotted English rugs were ablaze with flowers. Carpet weavers also accommodated those other denizens of the garden: butterflies, caterpillars, and other insects and even worms. The purple and yellow pansy, Queen Elizabeth's favorite flower, was particularly favored by the carpet makers. For their bright floral patterns, the English carpet weavers also drew on a type of embroidery known as "Turkey work," named after a long-pile embroidery stitch that resembled a handwoven Turkish knot. When Eastern trade routes were reopened toward the end of the sixteenth century, Oriental rugs were again imported. English carpet makers continued to produce their own floral patterns but now tailored them to fit Eastern designs.

## Outlandish Landscapes

**CHINTZ**

The end of the sixteenth century also saw the arrival in Europe of painted Indian cloths. They came by two routes: overland via the Levant to the Mediterranean, and by sea via the Cape of Good Hope to Lisbon, Antwerp, and London. England's first Indian cloths arrived as booty in the holds of captured Spanish ships, but its first legal imports were leftovers from the barter trade with the "spice islands" (the Moluccas). These arrived in the spice ship *Peppercorn* in 1613. So innocent were the social economies of the Moluccans that gold bullion was of no use as a medium of exchange. This left barter as the only practicable means of trade, and even with it the possibilities were limited. European goods were not coveted in the East. The only items perennially acceptable to the Moluccans were Indian piece goods, used for clothing, which they had first received from the Arabs who controlled the spice trade in the Middle Ages. Thus a three-cornered pattern of trade developed: bullion to India, textile piece goods to the Moluccas, and spices to Europe.

Most of the cottons brought to Europe in the spice ships are thought to have been cheap printed goods, but among them were dyed or "painted" wares in which the mordants or fixatives had been applied to the cloth freehand with a pen or brush. The painted cloths—known variously as *palampores*, *pintadoes*, or *chintes*—caught the eye of officials and directors of the East India Company, who were alert to the growing demand in Europe for decorative fabrics. Not only were the designs of the cloths novel, but their colors were brilliant and fast as well. European painted fabrics, by comparison, were dull and technically primitive. In England, for instance, a painted cloth was a piece of gum-soaked linen to which insoluble colors had been applied in much the same way as an easel painter applies pigment to canvas. The results were fugitive and the fabrics short-lived. Europeans also used dyes, but the metallic salts, or mordants, which react chemically with dyes to form insoluble colors were then unknown in Europe. Indian dyers, on the other hand, had known for centuries how to render colors completely fast and how to make dyes penetrate even resistant cotton fibers. When St. Jerome translated the Bible in the fourth century, he likened the lasting value of wisdom to the fastness of Indian dyes.

Yet despite their appeal to officials of the East India Company, painted Indian cloths failed in the marketplace. "They serve more to content and pleasure our friends," the directors lamented in 1643, "than for any profit [that] ariseth in sales." Though English tastes were predisposed to the exotic and the Oriental—at the founding of the East India Company, the "China shops" of the Royal Exchange were already flourishing—the traditional arts

A palampore, or painted cotton hanging, brought to England from India by the East India Company. Though appealing to officers of the company, Indian subjects were not popular with the English public. (By courtesy of the Board of Trustees of the Victoria & Albert Museum)

of India had little appeal to the West. Knowing virtually nothing of the geography of the Far East, Europeans had assumed there would be a uniform Oriental culture. When Sir Thomas Roe took up his appointment as James I's ambassador to the Mughal court in 1615, he was surprised and disappointed to learn that Chinese arts and crafts were not to be found in India. "I had thought all India a China shop, and that I should furnish all my friends with rarities; but this is not that part. Here are almost no Civil Arts, but such as the straggling Christians have lately taught."

If painted Indian cloth was to sell in European markets, evidently it

# Outlandish Landscapes

would have to conform to established tastes. The chief impediment to its popularity, as the London directors of the company saw it, was the "sad" color of the ground—a dark red—which they thought not "equally sorted to please all buyers." So in 1643 they instructed their agents in India to substitute white grounds for sad red ones. Sales increased, but still the market remained no more than lukewarm. Even so, the London directors were encouraged and decided on one further step: to send to the factors in India sample patterns, prepared in England, for Indian painters to copy. These included both English motifs and motifs "in the Chinese taste," that is, English motifs given a faintly Chinese flavor. "We now send you herewith enclosed," read a directive of 1662, "several patterns of Chints for your directions and desire you to cause a considerable quantity to be made of those Workes."

Branches and trees, which had long been features of English decoration, were prominent in the first patterns. "Now of late," wrote the London directors in 1669, "they are here in England, come to a great practize of printing large branches for hangings of Romes, and we do believe that some of our Callicoes painted after that manner might vent well, and therefore have sent you some patterns, of which we would have you send us some 2,000 pieces." At first, the Indian painters balked at the enforced change in habits, but when Jean Baptiste Tavernier visited India in 1670, he noted that many of them were painting calicoes from patterns given to them by European merchants. John Irwin, the preeminent modern analyst of "Oriental" styles, took wry pleasure in pointing out that the "Tree of Life" design, which European connoisseurs were fond of ascribing to Eastern symbolism, was in all likelihood rooted in the English and European predilection for trees. The curled, scroll-like leaves of the palampores probably owed more to the leaves of the verdure tapestries than to anything in the Indian tradition.

Though Indian cotton painters were good copyists, "the best Apes for Imitation in all the world," as the irreverent but admiring Edward Terry recorded in his diary in 1665, the results surprised the directors of the company. Painters, we know now, can paint only in their own idiom. The received image, as Sir Winston Churchill remarked, must go through the "post office" of the mind where it receives the stamp of the painter's temperament and culture. As a result, European subjects were thoroughly Indianized: Shepherds, rabbits, foxes, nosegays of English flowers tied in pretty ribbons —all were translated into forms familiar to the painter. The Hindu cotton painter, as bemused company officials repeatedly noted, painted "after his own manner," imposing upon both English and Chinese subjects his own decorative style and idiom. Pieces made "after the Chinese fashion" eventually turned up in China, where they were just as much of a novelty to the

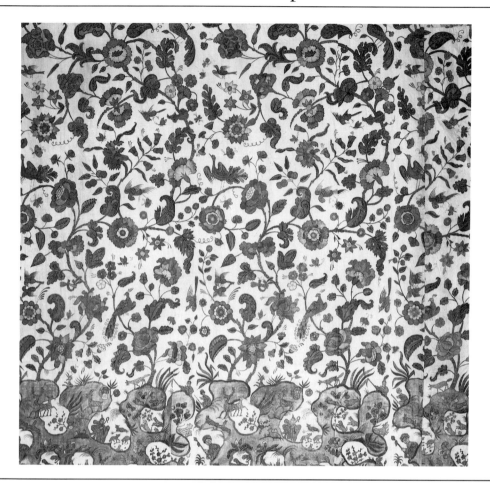

Painted cotton hanging made in India specifically for the English market. The weathered landforms are recognizably tropical, but the rabbits, foxes, deer, and stylized flowers were Indianized versions of English prototypes. (Samuel Putnam Avery Fund and Gift of Mrs. Samuel Cabot. Courtesy, Museum of Fine Arts, Boston)

Chinese as they were to the English. Eighteenth-century Chinese weavers copied some of them and so produced fabrics based on Indian patterns, derived from English originals, which expressed the European vision of the Orient. The circle had been closed. As the historian Hugh Honour remarked, there can have been few more bizarre incidents in the history of taste.

But no matter how hybridized the product, its reception in England exceeded the expectations of the directors. Within five years prices for painted cottons had increased by 20 percent and orders by 2,000 percent. The directors of the company clamored for more, and the more fanciful the better. Thus a 1694 order read: "10,000 Very fine . . . paintings, the finest can be made, done by the Neatest hands can be got, . . . as much variety of workes, new fancyes of the country's invention, nothing like English . . . the greatest part upon white grounds."

So insistent was the demand for chintz, which was used for both furnishings and clothing, that manufacturers of competing fabrics at home were alarmed. "From the greatest gallants to the meanest cook maids," wrote Pollexfen in 1697, "nothing was thought so fit to adorn their Persons as the fabrick from India! Nor for the ornaments of Chambers like India Skreens, Cabinets, Beds, or Hangings, nor for closets like China and lacquered ware." Fearing for its silk industry, France in 1686 imposed a heavy tax on all textiles imported from England and Holland (whether made there or not) and banned both the import of painted cloths from India and the home manufacture of Indiennes, their popular imitations. The prohibitions, maintained until 1759, stimulated the French wallpaper industry. Artisans accustomed to working in textiles turned to wallpaper, using their techniques of woodblock printing to produce the first landscape papers.

The English assault on imported Indian cloths began in 1700, but with a law so porous that it had virtually no effect on the trade. After a riot by the weavers of Spitalfields in 1719 a tougher and more effective law, forbidding the use of chintz in clothing as well as domestic furnishings, followed, but enough smuggled chintz still entered the country to meet the demand. As they sang in "The Weaver's Complaint":

> The merchant's all smuggle,
> And the trade's all a juggle,
> Carried on by leger-demain sir.

France, too, had a lively contraband trade, but Holland, with no domestic industries to protect, did not penalize imports. In England importation for reexport was legal, but much of the chintz brought into London supposedly destined for other shores never left the country. Many of the outbound ships got no farther than the Kent and East Anglian coasts, where the goods were furtively unloaded and brought ashore.

In India painted cottons were used chiefly for clothing; wall hangings were not part of the Indian tradition. The first hangings were made for Persians, who required them both for their palaces and houses in Persia and for their courts in the independent Islamic kingdoms in western India and the Deccan. Persians, like the English, held Indian artisans in disdain and brought in their own to teach Indians how to refine their techniques and produce motifs acceptable to Persian tastes. Once Persian styles had been mastered, the results could be very pleasing. In the 1600s the French traveler Tavernier was entertained at Delhi by the Great Mughal in a tent "lined with Masulipitan chintzes figured expressly for that very purpose with flowers so natural and colors so vivid that the tent seemed to be encompassed with real parterres."

In England, as in the Persian principalities, chintz was also used to decorate entire rooms. An inventory taken in 1641 referred to "a suite of hangings Consisting of Foure pieces of Indian Pantadoes & Curtaynes of the same suite for the same Roome, And a Canopy of the same suite with a valence thereunto. Pantadoe Carpetts for the same Roome." Chintzes used for hangings seem to have arrived not as sets of panels but in lengths to be cut up by the purchaser according to dimensions of walls to be covered. In his diary entry for September 5, 1663, Pepys noted that he had bought his wife "a chinte . . . that is paynted Indian calico for to line her new study which is very pretty." Chintzes to be cut up were composed of repeated patterns of plants or figures which some observers think might have been influenced by the design of Flemish verdure tapestries. Others see a resemblance between certain floral chintzes and the large flower heads and spiraling stems of Stuart embroidery.

European tastes are also evident in chintzes illustrating Indian labors. In Lady Mordaunt's house at Ashley Park, in 1665, John Evelyn saw hanging on a wall a "pintado full of figures great and small, prettily representing sundry trades and occupations of the Indians, with their habits."

The popularity of the bright, exotic fabrics from India inevitably influenced the design of European textiles. The poet John Taylor was simply responding to the popular demand for exotic subjects when, in verse written for James Boler's *Needle's Excellency*, he included patterns inspired by the wares of distant lands:

> Beyond the bounds of faithlesse Mahomet:
> From spacious China and those kingdomes East
> And from great Mexico, the Indies West.

Needleworkers who might previously have worked in monochrome were quickly won over to more colorful forms. Embroiderers in wool—crewel workers—whose patterns had originated in the free-flowing forms of Elizabethan blackwork, began to embroider birds with gaily colored plumage, and trees with lush, tropical leaves supported by buttress roots anchored in hummocky ground. "Crule," "crewle," or "croyl" was an inexpensive yarn of closely twisted long-fibered wool (worsted) which became the staple of seventeenth-century needleworkers. While the fortunes of the rural poor plummeted in the sixteenth and seventeenth centuries, the living standards of sheep rose dramatically. Enclosure of the wastes and commons resulted in more nutritious grasses, which in turn produced sheep with coarser and longer wool. Encouraged in part by the availability of worsted wools, English

# Outlandish Landscapes

women laid aside their stumpwork and, as Pepys noted, began making hangings and new "furniture" for beds.

Palampores also influenced the designs of printed cloths. As early as 1676 an Englishman, Will Sherwin, who had discovered a method of permanent dyeing, was given a patent to print on broad cloth in "the only true way of East India printing and stayning such kind of goods." In the eighteenth century English haberdashers, hoping to replace Indian fabrics with their own, offered to draw "India patterns" for their customers. English commerce with India was at its height between 1764 and 1775 when the basic inventions of the English cotton industry were made. As a result, nearly every well-to-do house in England contained Indian hangings made either at home or abroad. Best beds everywhere were hung with chintz and covered with pintado quilts, and no lady of fashion could hold up her head without a calico gown or, at the very least, an Indian shawl to wrap around her shoulders.

**CHINOISERIE**   Although India and the Near East intrigued Europeans, both regions were part of the known world, and interest in them, though great, was finite. Beyond India, however, and separated from it by mountains so high that the Great Flood had not covered them lay a land of immense size and untold riches. Europeans knew it as Cathay, and from the Middle Ages it had nourished European imaginations in ways that only unknown worlds can. Poets, Hugh Honour pointed out, were its only historians and porcelain painters its most reliable topographers. They alone could evince the beauty of its snowcapped mountains, its fruitful plains sprinkled with cities of dreaming pagodas, its streams spanned by delicate bridges, and its fleets of beribboned, finely wrought junks laden with cargoes of jade, porcelain, silk, green ginger, and delicately scented teas.

Like all places of reverie, Cathay was a land of perpetual spring and, for good measure, of giant peonies, chrysanthemums, and convolvulus whose blossoms were large enough to serve as hats and parasols. The inhabitants of this demi-paradise were small and neat and wore flowing robes of silk embroidered with gold. They lived in brightly painted latticework houses set in a natural landscape so picturesque that when laying out their gardens, Cathaians could do no better than reproduce it in miniature. Save for a few rustics who happily tended their flocks or sat somnolently on the backs of water buffalo, they knew nothing of work. Their true talent, Hugh Honour wrote, was for a serene, contemplative life.

The legend of Cathay was the gift of Marco Polo, who traveled extensively in Asia between 1271 and 1295, and of his chronicler Rustichello. Though master of several spoken Asiatic languages as well as his native Italian, Marco Polo could not write, and his remarkable tale, recorded by Rustichello—a practiced writer of romances—lost nothing in the transcription. It was also skewed by the eccentricities of its source. Marco Polo was a faithful reporter of things seen but an uncritical retailer of information acquired from others. As an observer and recorder, too, he was more than usually selective, ignoring everyday customs and habits in favor of the marvels he had seen or heard about. His tale was a recital of wonders, only half believed, but from it grew the European vision of the fabulous East.

Subsequent accounts of Cathay either confirmed or amplified the image. Friar Odoric of Pordenone, who was one of several Franciscan missionaries to travel in the Mongol empire in the fourteenth century, released only a few tantalizing details of his experience for fear that he would be disbelieved. He remarked on how the women's feet were bound, how the mandarins encouraged their fingernails to grow to extravagant length, and how the cormorant had been tamed and was used for fishing. Details such as these were bound to whet European appetites, but even more tantalizing were the details he refrained from giving on the grounds that they would seem "past belief" to those who "had not heard them with [their] own ears or seen the like." These, of course, flung wide the doors to imagination.

The third architect of the medieval vision of Cathay was an engaging mountebank who had never traveled beyond the Mediterranean. "Sir John Mandeville" was an Englishman, born and raised in Saint Albans, who allegedly made a journey to China in the 1320s. Thirty years later he wrote an account of it from memory. His book, *The Travels of Sir John Mandeville*, was an entertainment that cleverly combined what was already known about the Near and the Far East with fantasies that met medieval expectations of what awaited adventurers in unknown and antique lands. After a routine passage through the Mediterranean and Asia Minor, readers were taken across the land of the Amazons to the fabulous land of Cathay and the archipelago of islands which surrounded it.

"Mandeville" had genuine literary talent, and like many a bold mountebank he was lucky. No sooner had he presented his colorful fiction to a receptive public than the advancing forces of Islam cut off European routes to the Orient. Mandeville's hoax went undetected, and his book—translated into ten languages—was not only a medieval best-seller, but for two hundred years it was also regarded as the most authoritative work on the Orient. Copies of the book served as a fair medium of exchange in London, Bruges, and Paris, and itinerant merchants who gathered in these cities, so it was said, liked to listen to readings from it.

# Outlandish Landscapes

Circumstances conspired to protect the legend of Cathay even after the discovery of a sea route to the Orient early in the sixteenth century. Free commercial relations with China would quickly have shown that Chinese feet, though bound, were made of ordinary clay. But by confining European traders to coastal stations and sanctioning only a limited trade, the Chinese inadvertently perpetuated the myth of a lotus land on the far side of the world. Though on the threshold of Cathay, Europeans were allowed only mouth-watering glimpses of it through the barricades.

Objects that passed through the barriers and eventually reached the West confirmed the vision of Cathay as a land of ethereal delights. By sea via the Cape of Good Hope and overland by the silk routes came diaphanous silks, delicate porcelain vases, finely made lacquer cabinets, and sheets of hand-painted wallpaper. The wallpapers, usually arranged in sets of twenty or twenty-five nonrepeating panels each 4 feet wide and 12 long, were at first offered as gifts to Europeans at the conclusion of a sale. They took Europe by storm. No two papers were exactly alike, but the patterns, which followed established traditions in Chinese painting, fell into two categories: detailed studies of birds, insects, flowers, and foliage; and landscapes and scenes of daily life. A landscape might combine high peaks, rushing streams, and waterfalls with, in the foreground, gay gold and red pavilions and richly robed mandarins. The more detailed studies introduced Europeans to plants and flowers such as the lotus, the peony, the camellia, and the bamboo; and to Chinese varieties of birds such as the kingfisher, the heron, and the partridge. Individual panels were designed to fit together to form continuous scenes that might encompass an entire room.

The papers were painted in bright, attractive colors, and though the scenes lacked depth or perspective, each object was rendered with such fidelity that the effect was of great authenticity. They impressed no less a figure than Sir Joseph Banks, the renowned eighteenth-century explorer and naturalist. He noted in his journal (1770): "A man need go no further to study the Chinese than the China paper. . . . Some of the plants which are common to China and Java, as bamboo, are better figured here than in the best botanical authors that I have seen."

Scenes of daily life were commonly set in coastal cities as yet untouched by Europeans. Junks crowd waterways spanned by delicate bridges, and silk weavers and china makers ply their trades in busy city workshops. Papers showing the various stages in the production of pottery, silk, tea, or rice, the "factory papers" of the modern antique trade, were made specifically for export to Europe. Tea, which appealed enormously to European palates, was an especially popular subject, and papers showing how it began on cultivated hillsides and ended in city shops were assured of a market.

Detail from a Chinese landscape or export paper of scenes from rural life. So that figures could be rendered at a large scale and seen in detail — by European viewers — little effort was made to create a three-dimensional illusion of space. (Courtesy of Cooper-Hewitt, National Museum of Design, Smithsonian Institution/Art Resource, NY)

After the middle of the seventeenth century, Chinese products poured from the holds of the spice ships into the markets of London, Paris, and Amsterdam. Europeans fell on them, and a vogue for Orientalia swept the Continent. Demand far outran supply, and prices spiraled. Sensing a market for imitation Chinese wares, European craftsmen and craftswomen began to copy Chinese artifacts and the scenes found on them. The result was a new decorative style, "chinoiserie"—or in France, *lachinage*—which, like chintz,

# Outlandish Landscapes

An eighteenth-century export paper hung in the Chinese Parlor at the Henry Francis Du Pont Winterthur Museum. Chinese scenes offering details of landforms, animals, buildings, and the life and labors of the people were of endless fascination to Europeans. (Courtesy, The Henry Francis du Pont Winterthur Museum)

usually bore only a token relationship to the originals that had inspired it. John Evelyn recalled (1662) seeing in Paris a shop on the Isle du Palais which sold "all curiosities, natural or artificial, Indian or European, for luxury use such as cabinets [of lacquer], shells, ivory, porcelain, dried fishes, birds, pictures, and a thousand exotic extravagances."

In France, as elsewhere, the appeal of foreign objects and places owed something to the condition known as "Europamudigkeit," a sickness or weariness with Europe. Its comfortable victims, "Europamudes," suffered from nothing more serious than ennui. They were bored with a way of life, civilized and invariably easy, which for them lacked interest and zest. They sought relief in adventure and travel and, for those with neither the energy for the one nor the means for the other, in romantic interpretations of life in strange lands.

So admired were Chinese objects and motifs that to embroider, paint, or do lacquerwork "in the Chinese taste" or "the Indian manner" (ignorance of Far Eastern geography made the terms virtually synonymous) became fashionable pastimes. Caught up in the general enthusiasm, the needlewomen of England quickly began to imitate Chinese designs. In the middle of a quilt of brilliant colored silks, made by Sarah Thurstone in 1694, is a tiny figure who, apart from some familiar details such as oak trees and roses, stands alone in an alluring Oriental-looking landscape. Other embroideries, showing small patches of land rising like islands from a sea and crowded with figures, buildings, and trees, imitated the Chinese manner of landscape painting.

For models, needleworkers used imported Chinese embroideries, pattern books, and illustrations in books about China. The engravings of landscapes, plants, and birds in John Stalker and Henry Parker's *Treatise of Japaning and Varnishing* (1688) were used as much by embroiderers as by painters. The illustrations were based on specimens of imported lacquer, but wherever the proportions of these had been "lame or defective," the obliging authors "helped them a little . . . and made them more pleasant." For purists, authentic views of Chinese buildings and gardens were available in Dutchman John Nieuhof's *Embassy to the Grand Tartar*. The book occasioned great excitement when translated into English in 1669. Almost every fashionable library would have had its shelf of Orientalia. So great was the output of books on the Orient that in 1662 John Evelyn felt bound to declare that another volume on China would not be "to the purpose."

By 1700, chinoiserie tapestries were being woven in London, Paris, and Beauvais. One of the first London sets was a commission for Elihu Yale, founder of Yale College, who retired from the governorship of Madras in 1699. Each hanging consisted of a number of brightly colored scenes that showed Orientals riding, taking picnics, or making music among the giant trees of Eastern gardens. English and French paper manufacturers also began to copy Chinese wallpapers, and to meet the swelling demand, some even brought in Chinese artisans who were given some direction in European preferences.

In Europe, as in China itself, wallpaper was an inexpensive substitute for woven cloth hangings. Readers of the London *Gazette* in 1694 were invited to buy "strong paper hangings, with fine Indian figures in pieces of about twelve yds. long and about half an ell broad." By 1754 a London manufacturer, possibly John Jackson of Battersea, claimed to have improved on the originals: "These new invented paper hangings," he announced in the London *Evening Post*, "in Beauty, Neatness and Cheapness infinitely surpass any-thing of the like nature hitherto made use of, being not distinguishable from rich India [i.e., China] paper and the same being beautifully colored in pen-cil work and gilt."

The imitations varied enormously. Some of the papers were faithful to the originals, but others were improbable mixtures of European and Orien-tal cultures, clothes and landscapes sold under such labels as "Decor Chi-nois," "India Figures," and "Chinese Pieces." The most deviant designers were the French, who, according to Phyllis Ackerman, fabricated a world of diminutive Chinese—such as never existed—clothed them in amusing dis-tortions of Chinese costume, and set them down in strange scenes com-pounded of vague reports, fancy, or imagination. Chinoiserie papers were also made in America; in 1755 a Baltimore merchant offered "Mock India Pictures . . . all entire the manufacture of this country."

For many buyers, however, the "mock" papers were more appealing than the originals. In an order sent to a London supplier in 1738, Thomas Han-cock of Boston enclosed a fragment of chinoiserie wallpaper, "all that is left of a Room lately Come over here, and takes much in the town and will be the only paper-hanging for sale wh. am of the opinion may answer very well." He asked that the paper be "well Done and Cheap as Possible" and that it be made more beautiful by adding "more Birds flying here and there with some Landskips at the Bottom." Elsewhere in the letter he made clear that what was wanted were papers made in England rather than China. He described the wallpapers of a Boston friend, "Done in the same manner but much handsomer . . . made by one Dunbar in Aldermanbury." He specified, too, that the birds were to be peacocks and parrots, not herons and hawks.

By the end of the seventeenth century in England, entire rooms in mod-est merchant as well as gentry houses were being decorated in the Chinese style. There are frequent references to them in English letters. In 1682 John Evelyn recorded a visit to his "good neighbour Mr Bohun, whose whole house is a cabinet of all elegancies . . . in the hall are contrivances of Japan screens instead of wainscot. . . . The landskips of these skreens represent the manner of living, and Country of the Chinese." The Chinese style was also popular on the Continent, particularly in France. Rooms there were hung with printed cottons and linens, in the style of Chinese wallpapers, showing fragile buildings and large, flowering trees. Even classicists as staunch as the architect Jean-François Blondel had to give ground. Though opposed in principle to Oriental decoration, he conceded that in country houses Chinese and Indian plants and figures were the proper decor for the room "ou l'on passe pour prendre le caffe."

The fascination with things Oriental lasted only as long as the East re-

**Chinoiserie wallpaper, English, ca. 1770. The conical hills and the gnarled, dead tree were, like the two plants, designed to invoke an exotic landscape. The rider's mount has the tail of a horse but the head and neck of a camel. For many buyers the "mock" papers were more appealing than the originals. (By courtesy of the Board of Trustees of the Victoria & Albert Museum)**

mained distant and remote. The Reverend Archibald Alison, writing in 1792, found the explanation for the Chinese taste in the fact that "however fantastic and uncouth the forms of reality were, they were yet universally admired, because they brought to mind those images of Eastern magnificence and splendour, of which we have heard so much, and which we are always willing to believe because they are distant." But as the East drew nearer to Europe, the enchantment lent by distance diminished. Increased trade with the

## Outlandish Landscapes

Far East brought Europe enough artifacts to satisfy even the humblest collector of exotica. At the same time, European travelers to China began to question the European image of Cathay.

The first cracks in the image appeared in 1748 when Richard Warner, in his book *A Voyage around the World*, described in singularly uncomplimentary terms the rough treatment of Commodore Anson by the provincial officials of Canton. Anson had found the magistrates to be corrupt rather than serenely philosophical, the people thievish, and the tribunals crafty and venal. Later in the century Cathay received the gentle but damning censure of art. William and Thomas Daniell, who made *A Picturesque Voyage to India by Way of China* in 1784, and William Alexander, who traveled to Peking as the official draftsman in Lord Macartney's embassy in 1793, appreciated the picturesque qualities of the Chinese landscape but made no effort to romanticize or sentimentalize them. Exposed to the clear light of topographical truth, the legend of Cathay simply evaporated. Interest in Oriental wares survived only in England, where it depended on English dominion in India, and even here it was confined chiefly to textiles. Once the spell of the East had been broken, Oriental decoration could no longer fend off the attacks of the classicists. Incensed by what he considered the excessive love of things Chinese, John Shebbeare, in *Letters on the English Nation* (1756), opined that in a prudent society walls covered with Chinese paper "fill'd with figures which resemble nothing in God's creation . . . [would be prohibited] if only for the sake of pregnant women." In the same year the architect Isaac Ware, whose *Complete Body of Architecture* is said to have best represented contemporary architectural theory, advocated banning Chinese decoration. He thought it "mean, frivolous and shocking to the eye of science by its absurdity." Absurdity or irregularity also disturbed the engraver John Baptist Jackson. In the 1760s he castigated those "who chuse the Chinese manner [for preferring the] crooked, disproportioned and ugly [to] the strait, regular and beautiful."

# The Neoclassical Landscape

Though greatly attracted by distant places and exotic artifacts and plants, Europeans did not, of course, lose interest in their own. The landscape of home continued to appeal, and it vied with chinoiserie and chintz as a subject for decoration. Until the seventeenth century, interest in landscape had focused on gardens and the hunt. Gardens were of limited size, and, though not as tightly enclosed as they had been in the Middle Ages, they were still surrounded by trellis fences, hedges, or walls. Beyond the gardens lay hunting parks—themselves enclosed or fenced to ensure the privacy and preservation of the game—and the fields, fens, and moorlands. All these were still in their "native rudeness." Almost every county in England, as the social historians Sydney and Beatrice Webb noted early in this century, "had its hundreds or thousands of acres of 'moss' or swamp." Apart from the more refined pleasures of the hunt, the landscape beyond the garden and nearby meadows and fields was not looked to for aesthetic pleasure.

The barriers dividing garden from park and surrounding

country were broken down first in France. The instrument of their destruction was André Le Nôtre, the celebrated seventeenth-century landscape gardener. By making openings in hedges and walls and running avenues through the hunting parks, Le Nôtre drew the eye from the windows of the house across the garden and down the avenues that subdivided the park. In an age of discovery when horizons on earth and in the heavens were being set back, no scheme was too ambitious to be embraced and no park too large to be brought into immediate relation with the house. Le Nôtre's grandest conception, Versailles, was organized around a central axis that stretched as far as the eye could see.

**THE ENGLISH**

**LANDSCAPED**

**GARDEN**

From France the fashion for large-scale, comprehensive plans spread to England. When the tireless Celia Fiennes rode sidesaddle through England at the turn of the eighteenth century, she noted with meticulous care the details of the country seats she visited. She found a large number of "new built" houses and an even larger number of gardens and parks either newly planted or about to be developed. At Burghley House, in Northamptonshire, she was impressed with the park and its many rows of trees. She noted, "[The house] stands in a very fine park which is full of deer and fine rows of trees. On either side a very broad Glide or visto that looks finely to ye River and to the adjacent hills, a distance, both with fine woods."

In England, however, the French ideal of regimented nature was quickly challenged by the proposition that the alternative to a natural, and seemingly chaotic, world was not necessarily a symmetrical one. As woodland and fen retreated before an orderly network of fields and lanes, disordered nature began to appeal. Sir Henry Wootten in the seventeenth century and Lord Shaftesbury in the eighteenth both intimated that there might be virtue in irregularity. The roots of romanticism lay deep in European culture and society, but in England the catalysts for change were Franco-Italian painters. The sequence of events they triggered is well known.

After the Restoration (1660) the English embarked on Continental travel, and in Italy—the destination for all grand tours—they saw for the first time landscape paintings by Claude Lorraine, Nicolas Poussin, and Salvator Rosa. So pleased were they with the painted landscapes that on their return to England they used them as templates for reshaping their estates. The exemplars were Claude's dreamy, idealized interpretations of the Roman *campagna*, or open plain. In them cattle and sheep, unrestricted by hedges or

# The Neoclassical Landscape

fences, graze peacefully beside carefully tended glades or open, unthreatening woodland. Figures in the landscape do no work more onerous than shepherding, and they, like the animals and plants, are bathed in a radiant light. The land in golden age landscapes is almost never cultivated.

Reconstruction of the English estates began early in the eighteenth century. The first step was to remove from sight all walls and fences so that gardens and parks, as Horace Walpole put it in 1770, "might assort with the wilder country without." The enabling instrument was a fence placed at the bottom of a deep ditch, the renowned *haha*, which restricted the movements of animals but did not interrupt the view. Though different in form from Pliny's stepped box hedge, the haha was cousin to it. Like the stepped hedge, it signified that the garden was no longer a sanctuary and indicated a willingness to seek aesthetic satisfaction in the woods and fields beyond the garden. Sensibilities leapt the fences, as Horace Walpole remarked, "and saw that all nature was a garden." As in Roman Italy, a view across orchards and cultivated fields came to be regarded as one of the amenities of the house, a property that contributed to what Jane Austen would later describe as "English comfort." In *Emma* (1816) she used it to describe a view of a garden, bounded by a stone wall, beyond which lay farm buildings and a meadow enclosed by a bend of the river. "It was a sweet view, sweet to the eye and the mind. English verdure, English culture, English comfort."

In eighteenth-century England the way to appreciation of the wider landscape was smoothed by changes to the landscape itself. Landowners, aided by a Parliament that they controlled, were determined to eliminate the native rudeness of unimproved parts of the country. Common lands were enclosed, heathlands plowed and reseeded, swamps drained, and existing pastures improved. Land that formerly had been boggy, sandy, or "all horrid and woody" was transformed into a neat patchwork of fields and roads. By complementing these changes to the working landscape with new buildings and judicious plantings, a landowner might, as Joseph Addison remarked, "make a pretty Landscape of his own Possessions." In theory the two kinds of improvements held out the prospect of combining beauty and productivity, a union as appealing to English landowners as it had been to Roman ones, but in practice the demanding neoclassical eye all too often required the removal from sight of the instruments of production—barns, mills, farms, cottages, and even entire villages.

The corollary to admiration for the landscapes of Claude, and the Roman campagna on which they were modeled, was distaste for the formal French style. Addison's censure, delivered in the *Spectator* in 1712, is probably the best known: "Our trees rise in cones, globes and pyramids. We see the mark of the scissars upon every plant and bush." Addison dreamed of the charms of a seemingly wild garden: "A little wandering rill to run through it in the same manner as it would do in an open field, so that it generally passes through banks of violets and primroses that seem to be of its own producing." In an essay in the *Guardian*, written a few years later, Richard Steele took as his model the fruitful garden of Alcinoüs: How contrary to its simplicity, he exclaimed, was the modern practice of gardening. "We seem to make it our study to recede from nature." Alexander Pope, too, while pleading the case for an "artful wildness," took aim at the formal garden: "Tired of the scene Parterres and Fountains yield, / He finds at last he better likes a field."

Owners of formal gardens and estates took the censures to heart; down came topiary animals, pyramids, and balls, together with avenues of beech, lime, and elm, and up went artfully simple stands of trees separated by great swards of grass. The new landscape was pastoral incarnate: gentle slopes, lawns, fields, grazing animals, clumps of trees, and sinuous stretches of water. It might have been nature still, as Pope remarked, but it was nature simplified and "methodis'd." Only elements that "composed" were allowed into the picture; elements that did not were ruthlessly removed.

Though closer in appearance to wild nature than the formal French garden, the landscaped English garden was no more profligate of flowers. Following the example of landscape painting rather than embroidery, fashionable eighteenth-century gardeners concentrated on space and design, not color and pattern. Flowers and flowering shrubs were banished to the kitchen garden or hidden behind walls. Sir Thomas Hanmer allowed near the house only those flowers "such as grow very low"; the landscape architect Stephen Switzer, however, was for banishing flowers altogether, preferring a plantation of trees up to the very walls of the house to the presence of any borders worked in patterns. "Wherever Liberty will allow, I would throw open my Garden to all View, to the unbounded Felicities of distant Prospect and the expansive Volumes of Nature herself." Eyes were not to be balked by high walls, misplaced woods, and the "several obstructions . . . seen in too many places." To soften the transition from the formal garden to the wildness of the park, he also advocated (shades of Hadrian and the Vale of Tempe) that those parts of the garden most distant from the house be treated in a more "natural" manner.

# The Neoclassical Landscape

**ATTITUDES TO THE**

**COUNTRYSIDE AND**

**COUNTRY LIFE**

In addition to sweeping changes in the appearance of gardens, fields, and parks, there were notable shifts in sensibility and attitude to the countryside and country life. John Ray, the seventeenth-century naturalist, might have been able to praise people for "adorning the earth with beautiful cities," but the eighteenth century saw the beginnings of antiurban sentiment and, its corollary, idealization of the countryside. People did not pine for the countryside, the eighteenth-century critic Hugh Blair observed, so long as they lived on terms of daily familiarity with it. The taste for the pastoral depended upon the prior growth of towns, the shrinking of their gardens and orchards, and the disappearance of trees and flowers. Urban vices and nuisances were also beginning to make themselves felt, even though towns were still small. London, by far the largest of English cities, had a population of half a million in 1700, yet no part of the city was more than twenty minutes' walk from the country.

Although the appeal of the countryside was negative in part, most people had positive reasons for living in rural areas or making excursions to them. Increasingly, the countryside was seen as the place for relaxation and refreshment. By the mid-seventeenth century, country jaunts or "rambles" were a common form of relaxation, and by the mid-eighteenth century the keepers of inns and lodging houses in villages on the fringes of London profited from catering to crowds of weekend trippers from the city. Many prosperous merchants also built summer houses and garden pavilions in the rural suburbs and adjacent villages. In 1748 a Swedish visitor noted that scattered among the market gardens of Chelsea and Fulham were large brick houses belonging to London gentlemen and gentlewomen who went to them on Sunday afternoons for the sake of some country air; and in 1754 an essayist in the *Connoisseur* made fun of the little weekend villas in Turnham Green or Kentish Town to which London tradesmen would retire with their families "for the end and the beginning of every week."

For the wealthy, land itself was an attractive commodity. Farming was still the foundation of England's wealth, making land both a sound investment and a guarantor of social position. England, too, was the home of agrarian capitalism, where for the first time land could be owned without paternalistic obligations to laborers and tenants. The new concept of ownership was embodied in those two resonant eighteenth-century words: *property* and *improvement*. English landowners were as interested in the productivity and value of their estates as ancient Romans had been in their villas. They held to the classical notion that beauty in landscape and fertility were inseparable, and by doing so they revived the idea of "holy agriculture." The vision, for such it was, was perfectly expressed by Smollett in *Travels through France and Italy* (1766):

> I see the country of England smiling with cultivation; the grounds exhibiting all the perfection of agriculture, parcelled out into beautiful enclosures, cornfields, hay and pasture, woodland and common. . . . I see her meadows well-stocked with black cattle, her downs covered with sheep. . . . I see her farmhouses the habitations of plenty, cleanliness and convenience: and her peasants well fed, well lodged, well clothed, tall and stout, and hale and jolly.

Though the idea of a prosperous countryside and a contented peasantry acquired a particular resonance in the eighteenth century, love of productive land was, of course, much older. When, near the end of the sixteenth century, Ralph Sheldon built a house at Weston, in Warwickshire, he commissioned from the family looms at Barcheston a set of tapestry maps that evoked the charm and productivity of the midland counties. Based upon Christopher Saxton's Surveys of the Counties of England (1579), they presented in pictorial—as distinct from symbolic—form the towns, villages, manor houses, parks, and woodlands of the Shakespearean countryside, all set within borders of fruit and flowers. The inscriptions were hymns to fertility: "Hear hills do lift their heads aloft from whence sweet springs doe flow: Whose moistyr good doth firtil make the valleis couchte belowe. Hear goodly orchards planted are in fruite which do abounde Thine eye wolde make thine hart rejoyce to see so pleasant ground."

As well as being the chief source of England's wealth, the countryside was also the guardian of its virtue, or so it was perceived. A conspicuous theme in the literature of the seventeenth and eighteenth centuries was that countryfolk were not only healthier than townspeople, but more virtuous as well. Gray's plowman, like Horace's sturdy husbandman, lived a spotless, independent life in contented obscurity. The sentiment was international. In France, Rousseau pronounced (in 1750) that humanity's age of innocence had been its happiest and best and that civilization had been its ruin. Failing a return to simple and ennobling savagery, he advocated the pursuit of uncomplicated crafts, preferably rural ones. The Church, too, presented the country as a more uplifting place than the town. God, as seventeenth-century writers were fond of saying, had made the country, whereas humans made the town. City dwellers, noted a Jacobean preacher, "see for the most part but the works of men," whereas countryfolk "continually contemplate the works of God." When on a country walk in 1728, the young poet and cleric Henry Needler declared that his "thoughts naturally [took] a solemn and religious turn."

There was, of course, nothing in actuality to justify the idea of a morally uplifting countryside or of a contented and virtuous peasantry. Ordinary wage laborers buffeted, in the second half of the eighteenth century, by enclosures and the loss of common lands, high prices, and a declining demand for their services looked nothing like the idealized shepherds and plowmen of the rural idylls. Like most idylls, the cult of the countryside was an evasion of reality which evinced neither a genuine desire to live in the country nor a wish to understand its way or its work. At worst, the evasion took the form of elaborate fantasies and conceits. The simplest of these was the ornamental cottage, or *cottage orné*. By the middle of the eighteenth century, town dwellers had begun to idealize the country cottage. Uvedale Price, one of the most powerful arbiters of eighteenth-century taste, declared that the country cottage with its thatched roof, curling smoke, and roses around the door was "the most tranquil and soothing of all rural objects." In 1772 Queen Charlotte built a cottage in the woods at Kew, and by the end of the century many people of means were passing occasional weekends in cottages specifically built for this purpose and equipped to a degree of luxury unknown to country people. Thatching, climbing plants, and rustic verandas were, however, de rigueur, and if royal precedent may be taken as a barometer, so was naturalistic decoration. The walls of one of the rooms at Kew were painted with convolvulus growing up a trellis of canes.

Even more extravagant were the ornamental farms. The most celebrated was Wooburn Farm in Surrey, bought by Philip Southcote in 1735 and laid out to his specifications. Southcote's objective was to apply the principles of picturesque gardening to a working farm: to bring, as he put it, "every rural circumstance within the verge of the garden." When Thomas Whateley (*Observations on Modern Gardening*, 1770) visited Wooburn, he noted that there were seats on all the walks around the farm which gave onto views that were unfailingly elegant and agreeable. Hedges around the cornfields were planted with roses, woodbine, jasmine, and "every odoriferous plant whose tendrils will entwine with the thicket." In the corners of the fields where the plow could not reach were little clumps of all sorts of flowers. But the farm also invaded the garden. Even the most gay and gardenesque parts were likely to be grazed and cultivated. Cattle and sheep grazed on the lawns, and ducks and geese foraged in the ornamental shrubberies.

For betraying "more wealthy expense than is consistent with the economy of a Farmer, or the rusticity of labour," Horace Walpole dismissed Wooburn as a habitation more suited to nymphs and shepherds than farmworkers. Presumably, he would have been just as critical of the *fêtes champêtres* in which revelers dressed as Arcadian shepherds and shepherdesses sang and danced on the lawns before country houses. Mary Delany described one such "fairy scene" at a *fête champêtre* at Lady Betty Hamilton's in July 1774: "People in general very elegantly dressed: the very young as peasants; the next as Polonise; the matrons dominos; the men principally dominos and many *gardeners*, as in the Opera dances."

**18TH-CENTURY**

**INTERIORS**

Despite the appeal of confections such as ornamental farms and *fêtes champêtres*, fashionable taste in Georgian England leaned toward the classical and the restrained. New houses, like newly landscaped estates, tended to be elegant and graceful—unfussy.

In architecture, Palladianism ruled. Designed for the wealthier classes of the Venetian territory, Palladio's houses were of the size and shape required by the English for a country house. They also—an additional attraction for classically educated English—appeared to recapture the spirit of the Roman villa, then known only from description.

Inside the house, Palladian rules of harmony and proportion were considerably relaxed, but here, too, taste favored the plain and the unpatterned. Just as gardens "wrapt all in everlasting green" replaced knot gardens, so plain, unpatterned stuffs tended to replace detailed embroideries of flowers, fruits, insects, and birds. In decoration, as in landscape gardening, line and form took precedence over color and texture. When Lady Mary Coke visited Lord Bute's house in 1774, she reported that "almost all the rooms were hung with light green plain papers . . . while the chairs, beds and so on were chiefly of satin, light green and white, which had a very good effect." Chinoiserie and chintz, too, lost much of their former appeal in favor of less colorful materials. Lady Holland wrote in 1764: "I am rather changeable to be sure in those things [the decoration of the house] but tho whims and fripperies may have a run, one always returns to what is really handsome and noble and plain."

Yet in ordinary houses, as in ordinary gardens, flowers and floral patterns seem to have lost little of their appeal. Thomas Fairchild noted in 1722 that Londoners still furnished their rooms with basins of flowers and bough-pots, bought from countrywomen, "rather than not have something of the garden before them." Pots of boughs were popular decorations for unused fireplaces. All the gardening books explained how to grow plants and flowers indoors, and there were always flowers for sale in the London streets. Gardenless cockneys also hung cheaply made trompe l'oeil garden scenes outside their windows. John Evelyn, rich enough to have country property of his own, scorned them: "[The scenes are] painted projections of our cockney glades, which appear like gardens of paste-board and march-payne, and smell more of paynt than of flowers."

## The Neoclassical Landscape

**EMBROIDERY**

In embroidery, too, many people preferred figured material over plain for household decoration. Less hampered by a classical education than men, women still saw nature in detail. Embroidery, therefore, remained popular even if forced in new directions. Traditionally, it had been a garden art thriving on rich textures and dense, intricate patterning— the very characteristics that were missing from the new gardens. By the seventeenth and eighteenth centuries, plants had lost much of their emblematic meaning and, with it, some of their mystery and charm. Gone, too, in an empirical and scientific age, were many of their former medicinal and culinary uses. Flower and herb gardens still retained their visual appeal, but the old hieroglyphic and analogical reading of them had virtually stopped.

Though the disappearance of the knot garden deprived embroidery of its natural subject, embroiderers lost none of their zeal for covering exposed surfaces with needlework. It was said of Queen Mary, wife to William III (reigned 1689–1702), that "she was oftener seen with a skein of thread about her neck than attending to affairs of state." Nimble fingers stitched in assembly and visiting rooms, and "the very playhouses," so it was said, were "witnesses of their pretty industry." Gardens, too, remained popular subjects even though many of them had become formal and plain. English gardens in the French style were seldom as large as their Continental prototypes, and many of them were still within the range of the needleworker. The embroidered panels of the gardens at Stoke Edith, Herefordshire, which were still being worked on when Celia Fiennes made her last visit to the property in 1699, show their clipped yew trees, ponds, garden ornaments, and orangery.

Landscaped estates, however, were beyond the range of the embroiderer, and few attempted them. The new gardens were modeled after paintings, and a true test of a well-designed garden was whether a landscape painter would choose to paint it. William Kent, one of the first gardeners to work in the landscape style, had first been a painter. In 1783 it was possible for a French author to write: "The art of gardening consists entirely in making pictures on the ground by the same rules as one does on canvas." Gardens existed largely from middle distance to horizon; the chief requirement of the foreground was that it not interrupt the view. From the house, the eye was drawn outward to lawns, lakes, and pastures, not, as in earlier gardens, to adjacent beds, plants, shrubs, and trees.

More comfortable with vignettes than vistas, the embroiderer tended to seize on the "objects" used by the landscape gardener—temples, summer houses, monuments, bridges, ponds—and embroider these singly or arrange them into manageable compositions. When landscapes were attempted, back-

An orangery garden in one of a pair of embroidered hangings, formerly at Stoke Edith in Herefordshire, now at Montacute in Somerset. Plain turf and topiary work have replaced flowery knots, and the garden, though still enclosed, is open to the landscape. The formalism of the garden is matched by the classical facade of the orangery behind. (National Trust Photographic Library)

ground features such as sky or mountains were usually painted onto the ground in watercolor. The embroiderer's instinct was to fill the entire surface with pattern, but there was so much space in the new embroidery that Mary Delany felt bound to complain that it was "provoking to have the ground take up so much more time than the flowers."

The subjects chosen by embroiderers reflected prevailing attitudes to the countryside and to country life. Arcadian scenes were very popular. Shepherds and shepherdesses tending their flocks, peasants bending eagerly to their tasks, and windmills twirling merrily on hilltops could usually be found scattered throughout the house on chair covers, sofas, and wall panels. Pole screens, which shielded people from drafts or the heat of the fire, were ideal surfaces for needleworkers. The panels were flat, and like bed valances, they were never sat or lain upon. Any well-appointed eighteenth-century sitting room would have had several of them so that each member of the company could be protected.

Embroidered pictures of houses were also popular. Country houses, to borrow a phrase from the English historian Raymond Williams, were the

# The Neoclassical Landscape

A tea party in the second, and smaller, of the two Stoke Edith hangings. A garden, wrote the retired diplomat Sir William Temple, "ought to lie to the best parts of the house . . . so as to be but like one of the rooms" out of which one steps into another. By the eighteenth century, garden houses, like the semicircular one in the hanging, had replaced leafy arbors that were sometimes damp and drafty. (National Trust Photographic Library)

visible centers of the new social system. If well run and self-sufficient, they, and their estates, were also a microcosm of the mercantilist state beloved of eighteenth-century economists. No portrait or sporting piece seemed complete without its country house. Embroiderers produced nothing quite as iconic of the eighteenth-century sense of property as Gainsborough's painting *Mr and Mrs Andrews* (ca. 1748–50), but sewn portraits of country houses and their proud owners adorned many a wall. The master and mistress, wearing courtly dress, usually stood in a lawn or garden in front of the house.

When writing about eighteenth-century embroidery, Rozsika Parker, a modern historian, concentrated on an elaborate "six leaft skreen" embroidered in the 1720s by Lady Julia Calverley. The size of the work—each of the leaves is nearly 6 feet high and 2 feet wide—and the care with which it was recorded by her husband and transported by her son testify to its importance to her family. But the screen was chiefly valued, Parker avers, not as the work of a wife and mother but as a representation of rural life which the family wanted—and needed. The theme of the Calverley screen, like the

**Pastoral scene, 1761. Embroidered pictures of substantial houses and prosperous estates were icons of the eighteenth-century sense of property. (All rights reserved, The Metropolitan Museum of Art. Gift of Irwin Untermyer, 1964 [64.101.1359])**

themes on countless chairbacks, sofas, pole screens, and wall panels, was Virgilian; the motifs, in fact, have been traced to Francis Cleyn's illustrations for Ogilby's translation (1654) of Virgil's *Eclogues* and *Georgics*. By combining classical and contemporary English scenes, Lady Calverley was able to suggest that English rural life was timelessly harmonious. A piping shepherd of Arcadia inhabits the same world as an English plowman; classically garbed figures stroll over rolling hills while below them a basket maker bends over his work, and a nobleman gallops in pursuit of a stag. There are references to the Civil War, but so oblique that they present no threat to the reassuring image of security and plenty, ease and social control.

An alternative to Arcadian imagery, which became popular in both the fine and decorative arts of the second half of the eighteenth century, was—the phrase is John Barrell's—the "jolly imagery of Merry England." Farmyard scenes were popular subjects for the needle and the brush. Though ostensibly realistic, they were as reassuring as Arcadian scenes and just as misleading. In the actual countryside, peasants did not labor happily or share in the good life. Deprived by enclosure of their customary rights on the commons and wastes, and "eaten up" by sheep, they were the first victims of agrarian capitalism. In England, as John Barrell put it in *The Dark Side of the Landscape* (1980), a money economy had replaced a moral one.

The vogue for Arcadian images affected even pioneer America. In the

Needlework screen by Lady Julia Calverley, 1716. The vision is Arcadian despite oblique references to the Civil War in some of the Calverley screens. In this screen, a shepherd guards his flock, and peasants make baskets and repair plows in a countryside that is both peaceful and productive. (National Trust Photographic Library)

"Fishing Lady" or "Boston Common" embroideries, young women, one of whom is sometimes fishing serenely, are courted by elegant young men in an idealized Boston Common landscape. The embroideries, fifty-eight in all, are thought to have been inspired by English pattern books and made by young women of prosperous New England families who may well have attended Boston finishing schools in the second half of the eighteenth century. The largest of them were framed and hung over mantels as ornamental "chimney pieces."

The stately house and garden was also a favorite American subject. Just as English tastes in landscape crossed the Atlantic, so too did the English sense of property and prospect. But in North America the same forms did not always carry the same associations. Whereas in England sweeping lawns and extensive pastures were in part nostalgic reminders of a pastoral golden age, in the United States they were symbols of material progress. In a continent where the forest was thick and rank, a clearing was a hard-won luxury, a successful transformation of the wilderness. Houses pleased for similar reasons. As well as signifying social position and professional or mercantile success, they stood for order and security. In the eighteenth century, the eastern seaboard was still a pioneer region where a soundly made, classically proportioned Georgian house standing square to the wilderness would have reassured settlers. Symmetry, order, and proportion, as landscape gardener Andrew Jackson Downing would note a century later, were critical underpinnings of the settlement:

> With the perception of proportion, symmetry, order and beauty . . . comes that refinement of manners which distinguishes a civilized from a coarse and brutal people. So long as men are forced to dwell in log huts and follow a hunter's life, we must not be surprised at lynch law and the use of the bowie knife. But, when smiling lawns and tasteful cottages begin to embellish a country, we know that order and culture are established.

As in England, it became fashionable to own a picture of one's country house, and by the middle of the eighteenth century traveling decorative painters, many of whom had come from England, were offering owners "draughts of their houses in colours or India ink" and "perspective views of gentlemen's country seats." Houses were also popular subjects in colonial embroideries. Merchants, lawyers, and landowners pose with obvious pride before their houses and gardens and even their barnyards and gardeners' cottages. A sentence in a letter to London, written in 1737 by the prosperous merchant Thomas Hancock, might well have served as the caption to an embroidered picture of his house on Boston Common: "My Gardens all Lye on the South Side of a hill with the most beautiful Assent to the top and its

# The Neoclassical Landscape

The vogue for the pastoral affected even pioneer America. In this "Fishing Lady" or "Boston Common" embroidery, young men court young women in an idealized landscape. (Courtesy, The Henry Francis du Pont Winterthur Museum)

allowed on all hands the Kingdom of England don't afford so Fine a Prospect as I have both of land & water."

Hancock built his handsome mansion in 1737, just below the summit of Beacon Hill, and dismayed his friends by his independent move from the fashionable end of the town to the undeveloped pasturelands beside the common. Neither money nor effort was spared to make it a dwelling place suitable for Boston's richest merchant. Decorations and furnishings were brought from England, "all to be very rich and beautiful," as were shrubs and trees: "Yewes, Holly and Jessamyne Vines to Beautifie a flower garden." Downstage center in the embroidery, Thomas Hancock and his wife contemplate the view over a wall of granite and freestone.

Houses and gardens were also favorite subjects for samplers. Initially these were practice and reference sheets (*exemplars*) for showing a variety of stitches and panels, but by the eighteenth century they were decorative forms in their own right. The sampler pictures and the earnest and didactic texts that usually accompanied them were often framed and hung on walls. Both English and American sampler makers were inclined to select imposing and elegant houses; most of the sampler makers would have come from good houses, and even those who had not would still have been attracted by the best houses in the village. Common salt-box or gambrel-roofed houses seldom appeared in American samplers. The subjects in virtually all cases were imposing Georgian mansions, frequently—for good measure—built of solid brick.

The embroidered picture, of which the framed sampler is an example, was the most characteristic type of needlework of the later eighteenth century. It was an attempt—misguided, as historians of embroidery see it—to emulate fine art. Embroidery began its "retreat" into the picture frame in the seventeenth century and capitulated in the second half of the eighteenth when a taste for light and elegant furniture—Hepplewhite and Sheraton— called for coverings that were plain and simple rather than fussy and ornamental. Unable to oblige, needleworkers turned most of their attention to decorative pictures.

The most refined form of embroidered picture was the needlepainting. By simulating the brush strokes of oil painters, professional or semiprofessional embroiderers were able to make copies of actual paintings. Needlepainting had no greater admirer than Arthur Young, the great agricultural reformer. On one of his rural rides through the northern counties of England, he saw, in York, "copies of several capital paintings worked by Miss Morret, a lady of most suprising genius." They included landscapes by Zuccarelli, Gaspard Poussin, Rubens, and Salvator Rosa, all of which Miss Morret had endowed "with beauty of a most surprising and pleasing nature." Dr. Johnson was no less pleased with the needlepaintings of Mary Knowles, whom he identified in a letter to a friend as a lady who worked "sutile pictures in needlework."

Rather than attempt copies of paintings, domestic embroiderers simply used paintings as sources of graphic ideas. Popular subjects were the hunt, inspired in particular by the paintings of John Wootton (1682–1764), and scenes of rural life after paintings by Gainsborough, Francis Wheatley, and George Morland. Morland was particularly popular, and sanitized prints of his paintings were widely available; in them thatched cottages had been subtly repaired, rustic complexions cleared, and family relationships harmonized.

Pictures of the respectable, or "deserving," poor at play or sitting contentedly around the family hearth served several purposes. Like the apologias, in the form of essays, tracts, and sermons on the poor, which poured off the eighteenth-century presses, they suggested that a modicum of poverty was inevitable—thus justifying the replacement of a paternalist by a capitalist economy—and that it could be borne, or compensated for, by industry, thrift, and the enjoyment of simple pleasures. In other words, they reassured the propertied classes that the poor could be as happy as the swains of Arcadia, and their lives as delightfully simple and enviable. Morland's paintings also appealed to eighteenth-century needlewomen because they

# The Neoclassical Landscape

**Hunting scenes, after paintings by John Wootton (1678–1765), were popular subjects for embroiderers and tapestry weavers. The mansion house in the background of this embroidery was added by the embroiderer. (All rights reserved, The Metropolitan Museum of Art. Gift of Irwin Untermyer, 1964 [64.101.1356])**

expressed humane concern; women who copied them acquired virtue by association and at the same time exonerated their craft from any taint of vanity and selfishness.

As well as copying paintings, embroiderers also made designs directly from nature. Sketching from life had become a feminine accomplishment, and by going directly to their subject embroiderers felt equal to oil painters. An interest in botany was expected of every eighteenth-century gentlewoman; no embroiderer, Mary Delany noted, could afford to be without an interest in gardens and plants. Systems of classification which depended upon the sexual characteristics of plants, surprisingly, were no deterrent. In

*Cherry Ripe*, after a painting by Francis Wheatley, last quarter of the eighteenth century. Original mezzotint, partly cut out and applied upon painted and embroidered silk. Pictures of the rural poor living in harmony and evident contentment were part of an elaborate myth that shielded the moneyed and propertied from the less agreeable consequences of capitalism. (All rights reserved, The Metropolitan Museum of Art. Gift of Irwin Untermyer, 1964 [64.101.1357])

# The Neoclassical Landscape

the 1780s Queen Charlotte took lessons from William Aiton of Kew and encouraged her daughters to follow her example. "There is not a plant in the gardens of Kew," wrote Robert Thornton, "but has either been drawn by her gracious Majesty, or some of the Princesses." Thornton described the *Botanical Magazine*, launched in 1797, as "a drawing book for ladies," and John Claudius Loudon, the renowned nineteenth-century gardener and garden writer, remarked that to complete the coloring of the partly colored *Botanical Cabinet* (1803), and add notes to the margins, "would be a charming and instructive female exercise." Loudon regarded botany as a study "peculiarly calculated for young ladies."

By the end of the eighteenth century, women were so closely identified with gardens that the association gave rise to a new kind of picture, the lady in a garden, usually embroidered in silk. In conventional embroidery, the most colorful expression of the keen female interest in gardens and plants was the "landscaped" dress: "The bottom of the petticoat [had] brown hills covered with all sorts of weeds, and every breadth had an old stump of a tree . . . round which were twined nasturtiums, ivy, honeysuckles, periwinkles, convolvuli and all sorts of twining flowers." The wearer was the duchess of Queensberry and the observer the eagle-eyed Mary Delany.

**TAPESTRY AND**

**WALLPAPER**

Most large eighteenth-century houses still had tapestries hanging in at least one of their principal rooms, but as decorations tapestries had lost their former preeminence. Favored subjects were the hunt and, as in embroidery, country pleasures, pastimes, and labors. Country scenes were often in the manner of David Teniers the Younger and Jean-Antoine Watteau, the popular Flemish and French painters. Teniers was best known for his peasant scenes, and tapestries based on them were known simply as "Teniers." Watteau became known as a painter of *fêtes galantes*, or *fêtes champêtres* in which finely, and sometimes extravagantly, dressed young people idle away their time in dreamy, pastoral settings. The English landscaped garden, *jardin anglais*, which had crossed the channel, was tailor-made for rural idylls.

The hunting scenes presented hunters, horses, and dogs in wide, airy landscapes. The new quarry was the fox, which had ousted the stag in the affections of hunters once the protective fences around the parks had been taken down. So coveted was the fox that, in newly enclosed landscapes where the natural cover had been grubbed up, hunting landlords planted gorse covers and spinneys where foxes might hide. In England, the smaller workshops that were still active made tapestries after the paintings of John

An early eighteenth-century English tapestry in the style of the Flemish painter David Teniers the Younger. In this adaptation the emphasis is on the occupations of the workers, not — as in Teniers' paintings — their pleasures. The work, however, is by no means onerous. (All rights reserved, The Metropolitan Museum of Art. Bequest of Mary Anna Palmer Draper, 1915 [15.43.312])

Wootton, a popular painter of hunting and racing scenes and, according to some, the father of English landscape painting. In many of Wootton's hunting pieces, the landscape backgrounds received as much attention as the hunters and horses.

Though tapestry weavers were more at home with prospects and vistas than were embroiderers, they, too, were presiding over a declining art. By raising easel painting above all other arts, Renaissance societies gave painters license not only to design tapestries but also to deny weavers freedom of interpretation. As a result, flat, nonperspective patterns were rejected in favor of open landscapes with low horizon lines and large skies. By the eighteenth century tapestries were not much more than woven imitations of paintings, and, for good measure, they were usually surrounded by borders that simulated carved picture frames. Weavers could represent the prospects

# The Neoclassical Landscape

and views demanded by eighteenth-century patrons, but large skies and empty spaces were not natural subjects for them.

By the end of the century, demand for tapestries had dwindled almost to nothing. The great Flemish workshops decayed and died; the last loom in Audenarde stopped working in 1772, and the last atelier in Brussels closed its doors in 1794. Existing tapestries were taken down and stored in attics, if they were lucky. If not, they were cut into pieces or destroyed. Older tapestries seem to have suffered most; in the century of Enlightenment things medieval were despised. Most of the hangings in France's royal furniture repository were burned by ministerial decree—but only after the gold threads, straps, and linings had been removed.

Though tapestry's ills were chiefly internal, its decline was precipitated by the growing popularity of rival wall coverings that were lighter, brighter, and more adaptable. Painted and printed fabrics, wallpaper, and paint were less expensive than tapestries and just as effective. They could be adapted to all tastes, they did not harbor dust, and they were impervious to the smells of food. Moreover, thanks to tighter windows and walls, coal-burning grates, and smaller rooms that were easier to heat, tapestries were no longer essential insulation. Around 1720, hearths were made narrower and deeper, mantels lowered, and chimney shafts curved. The changes increased the draft, improved combustion and heating, and virtually eliminated smoke. Domestic-scale rooms became appreciably warmer, but, by modern standards, they were still not warm.

Least expensive and most adaptable of the alternative coverings was wallpaper, which, from 1750, could be pasted as well as tacked onto walls. One London manufacturer advertised in 1737 that he could provide "fine hangings to match any Needlework, shaded in the most beautiful manner." By "flocking," or covering the surface of the paper with shreds of wool, wallpaper could also be given the look of tapestry. The demand for wallpaper so depressed the demand for tapestry that in the late 1750s Horace Walpole thought there would be a chance of affording the latter "in [a] country where People all disdain tapestry, because they hear that Paper is all the fashion." Wallpapers could be used, as today, as a fixed wall decoration, or they could be pasted onto canvas fixed to battens. As such, they were moveable. Advertisements in Paris newspapers offered "rooms" of such hangings for sale.

In England, colored, block-printed wallpapers were available in quantity from 1746 when John Baptist Jackson opened a factory in Battersea. His offerings were all-embracing: "landscapes after Salvator Rosa, Claude Lorraine, views of Venice by Canaletti, copies of all the best painters of the Italian, French and Flemish schools, in short every Bird that flies, every Figure

Forest scenery and a Peak District landscape on the walls of a room in Drakelowe Hall, Derbyshire. The painter was Paul Sandby, the celebrated eighteenth-century watercolorist. (By courtesy of the Board of Trustees of the Victoria & Albert Museum)

# The Neoclassical Landscape

that moves upon the Surface of the Earth from the Insect to the Human, and every Vegetable that springs from the Ground, whatever is of Art or Nature, may be used for fitting up and furnishing Rooms."

**WALL PAINTINGS**

The new confidence in the world beyond the garden and the hunting park was also expressed in wall paintings. The second half of the eighteenth century saw a revival of the Roman practice of covering walls with paintings so as to create an illusion of unenclosed space. French walls were painted with treed landscapes, and ceilings with blue sky and clouds. Parallels could be found all over Europe. England's most notable examples were at Norbury Park, Surrey, and Drakelowe Hall, Derbyshire. At Norbury Park, in the early 1780s, a room was painted to look as if it were a pergola in a wooded landscape. The Reverend William Gilpin described it as "a bower or arbour, admitting a *fictitious* sky through a large oval at the top, and covered at the angles with trellis-work, interwoven with honeysuckles, vines, clustering grapes, and flowering creepers. . . . The sides [were] divided by slight painted pilasters, appearing to support the trellis roof; and open to four views." To heighten the illusion of being in an arbor, painted light was made to simulate natural light almost exactly. Gilpin wrote at length of how exquisitely an autumn atmosphere had been evoked and how, when the natural hour corresponded to the hour represented, the coincidence of artificial and natural light was so close that "the landscape, both within and without the room, [appeared] illumined by the same sun."

To complete the illusion of a room without walls, the painted views were made to accord with the actual one, visible from a bow window. The house at Norbury lies on a steep hill so the foregrounds of the painted views on the two principal walls were allowed to slip away, giving the impression that the room was an arbor overlooking a valley. Below the walls, on the floor, was a green carpet that looked like an extension of the lawn outside the bow window. Close-cut lawns in the nineteenth century were known as *tapis verts*.

The room at Drakelowe Hall offered two landscapes as well as the actual one seen through a large window. It, too, had a literary admirer. "Sir Nigel [Gresley]," wrote Anna Seward in 1794,

> hath adorned one of his rooms with singular happiness. It is large, one side painted with forest scenery, whose majestic trees arch over the coved ceiling. Through them we see glades, tufted banks, and ascending walks, in perspective. The opposite side of the room exhibits a Peak valley: the front shows a prospect of more distant country, vieing with the beauties of the real one, admitted, opposite, through a crystal wall of window, the whole breadth of

the apartment. Its chimney-piece, formed of spars, and ores, and shells, represents a grotto. Real pales, painted green, and breast-high, are placed within a few inches from the walls, and increase the power of the deception. In these are little wicket gates, that, half open, invite us to ascend the seeming forest banks. The perspective is so well preserved as to produce a landscape deception little inferior to the watery delusion of the celebrated panorama.*

*A bird's-eye view of Edinburgh, by Robert Barker, painted as a continous picture within a circular hall.

# Nineteenth-Century Villas

n 1841 a woman wrote to the *Ladies Magazine of Gardening* to ask for guidance in planting a "geometrical flower garden with the *gayest* and *brightest* colours." Form and color had returned to the garden. Fifty years earlier a public declaration of this sort could not have been made. Yet by the end of the eighteenth century disgruntled property owners were beginning to complain privately of gardens so "natural" that they were indistinguishable from the surrounding countryside. Like the English connoisseur and poet Richard Payne Knight, they wished that "vary'd tints and forms would intervene to break [the] uniform, eternal green." They took heart from Humphry Repton, the first notable landscape gardner to challenge the inviolability of grass, and began to reorganize their gardens. Flowers were removed from the decent shelter of walls and replanted in formal beds beside the house. Terraces were built to keep lawns at bay, and trellises festooned with roses, jasmine, and honeysuckle were eagerly brought back. The relief was general, but no group sighed more audibly than the growing middle class, whose

surburban properties were too small to be landscaped in the eighteenth-century manner.

Only in the United States did openness prevail. The dislike of perimeter fences and hedges, which were considered unneighborly, and of banks of trees, which were uncomfortable reminders of the primeval forest, meant that houses in the new suburbs could still be set in a continuous greensward interrupted only by shrubs or beds of flowers. "Smiling lawn" stretched from corner to corner of the new surburban communities.

Pressures to change the form of the garden also came from without. While the ingredients of eighteenth-century garden design were becoming fewer and plainer, the number and variety of plants available to gardeners increased dramatically. Plants poured into Europe from every corner of the world, and thanks to the invention of a tightly glazed case by the eponymous Dr. Ward, their safe transportation could be guaranteed. From China came wisteria, peonies, and chrysanthemums; from Mexico the dahlia; from Central America the fuchsia; and from South Africa lilies and semisucculent pelargoniums. England was the largest receptacle. It had the most extensive colonial empire, enterprising plant hunters, and merchant and military ships that combed the seven seas. Few of these could not make room for rare or valuable plants.

In greenhouses and conservatories professional plant collectors and enthusiastic amateurs built up a great reservoir of species which was bound to spill upon the gardens of the nineteenth century. By 1770, Princess Augusta had managed to squeeze 3,400 species into her exotic garden at Kew; next door, in the fashionable garden in the grounds of Richmond Lodge, a fastidious Capability Brown limited himself to a mere eight. As the numbers of exotics grew, so did the desire to show them off. To satisfy the desire meant breaking the monopoly of the lawn.

The first step, taken by Humphry Repton, was to make shrubberies from the hardier American species. Then, in what is generally regarded as one of the strangest episodes in the history of gardening, the imported annuals were "bedded" out in the formerly pristine lawns. During the summer months, thousands of small, brilliant annuals were planted in densely patterned beds, reminiscent of Elizabethan knots, set into the expanses of lawn around the house. Though the beds were destroyed by the first frost and had to be replanted in the spring, the *Florists' Manual* could still report, in 1816, that "a flower garden is now become the appendage of every fashionable residence." By drawing the eye toward particular beds, shrubs, and trees rather than across the land, Victorian gardens were no longer vistas.

Not even the United States, where gardening on balance had been more practical than decorative, escaped bedding out. The way had been prepared

# Nineteenth-Century Villas

by the development of greenhouse culture in the first half of the nineteenth century and by a spate of small gardening books that insisted on the importance of floriculture as an aid to the refinement of manners, the happiness of the family, and the embellishment of the home. What will tend more to the cheerfulness of the home and the contentment of the family, wrote J. T. C. Clark in 1856, than a flower garden filled with beautiful flowers, "elevating and purifying the soul of the beholder?" Bedding out, or the "modern style," as it was called, became popular after the Civil War, just as it was beginning to fade in England. Its chief advocate was Peter Henderson, of New Jersey, and its chief practitioners the owners of new suburban properties. In *Practical Floriculture* (1869), which he wrote for commercial florists, Henderson declared that for a truly grand effect he had found nothing to surpass the ribbonlike plantings at Crystal Palace in London and at the Jardin des Plantes in Paris. The response to the new style was so favorable that Henderson wrote a second book for amateur gardeners. *Gardening for Pleasure*, which appeared in 1875, concentrated on flower beds; lawn making and shrub and tree planting Henderson left to landscape gardeners.

**BERLIN**

**WOOLWORK**

These changes to the garden were immediately echoed in decoration. Embroidery, the traditional garden art, was first to respond; intricate patterning and attention to detail were its stock in trade. Victorian women, too, had been instrumental in the revival of flower gardens. J. T. C. Clark addressed his flower-garden directory particularly to "the LADIES" of America. Prince Pückler-Muskau in 1828 attributed the beauty of English gardens to the "genius" of women and their "taste for the embellishment of *home*." In an 1850 issue of the *Villa Companion*, Mrs. John Claudius Loudon declared, "There is scarce such a thing to be found as a lady who is not fond of flowers." Her own *Ladies Companion to the Flower Garden* sold more than twenty thousand copies between 1848 and 1879. To encourage readers to translate fondness for flowers into active gardening, she used the example of embroidery as naturally as any Renaissance writer on gardens. Any woman "who can work or embroider patterns," she averred, had the skill to lay out a flower garden.

Practices then fashionable in needlework were so well suited to representation of the new gardens that Mrs. Loudon, who was also the editor of the *Ladies Magazine of Gardening*, could answer the question about ways of making geometrical arrangements of bright and gay flowers with an allusion to embroidery: "The situation having been chosen, the ground must be levelled, and the plan, if complicated traced upon it. Having divided the plan into an equal number of squares by lines drawn on the paper, copy what is found on a large scale in every square. This is difficult to describe, but it will be easy in practice to anyone who has been accustomed to copying worsted work patterns drawn on Berlin paper."

Berlin worsted or "woolwork," as it was popularly known, was the latest enthusiasm in embroidery, and it had, as the countess of Wilton noted, "quite . . . usurped the place of the various other embroideries which have from time to time engrossed the leisure moments of the fair." Brightly colored Berlin woolwork was spread over tables, chairs, stools, pianos, screens, and walls in an effort, Virginia Woolf suggested in her novel *Orlando* (1928), to dispel the great cloud that during the nineteenth century seemed permanently suspended over the British Isles. Cold, moist air found its way into every house, and to defend against it, walls and furniture were covered with woven or embroidered cloth, rugs were strewn on floors, and beards grown on faces; nothing was left bare.

Berlin patterns were laid out on squared paper, each tiny square representing a stitch. Historians of embroidery dismiss woolwork as the equivalent of painting by numbers, but it was uncannily suited to representing the geometry of early Victorian gardens. By using a stitch similar to one used in stumpwork, needleworkers could also reproduce the striking three-dimensional effects of "panel planting," in which groups of plants were slightly elevated above the "groundwork," or general level of the bed. But the essence of woolwork was mathematical precision. Plants in the new beds were laid out in geometrical patterns as complex as those in any of the earlier knots or parterres. But there comparison ends. The new bedding plants were far more colorful than the old, most being recently introduced exotics raised in hothouses during the winter.

One of the architects of the new designs, Joseph Paxton, was also the designer of a mammoth greenhouse, the "Great Stove," on the Chatsworth estate of the dukes of Devonshire. According to Mrs. Earle, a garden writer of the time, Paxton used old patterns from Italy and France to design his beds, filling them "as ha[d] never been done before," with cuttings of tender exotics kept under glass all winter. A formal garden planted with brightly colored flowers of roughly the same height ought to look, Mrs. Loudon remarked, like a Turkish carpet. The style, not unexpectedly, came to be known as "carpet bedding," and it first became popular in the 1830s just as Berlin patterns and wools were becoming readily available. The most suitable plants were dwarf varieties with small colored leaves and succulent plants that form rosettes of leaves close to the soil. The designs were first drawn to scale on paper, as in any piece of needlework, and then transferred to the finely raked beds with pegs, string, and T squares.

Carpet bedding was prodigal of plants; on average, four thousand were

# Nineteenth-Century Villas

needed to cover a thousand square feet of ground. In 1886, four beds in a private garden at Long Branch, New Jersey, held one and a half million plants, arranged so "artistically" that at a distance they might be mistaken for carpets laid out to air on a lawn. So effective was the "floral rug" that an elderly farmer and his wife, passing during a heavy rainstorm, are said to have driven in to warn the servants to lift the carpets before they were ruined. The story, no doubt, is apocryphal, but the gardens were so appealing that they attracted tens of thousands of visitors annually.

The connections between carpet bedding and Berlin woolwork remained remarkably close for about fifty years; changes of fashion in flowers, colors, and arrangements appeared in each simultaneously as if, so Thomasina Beck maintained in 1979, by some curious cross-fertilization. At first the embroidered flowers tended to be old favorites such as roses, auriculas, pansies, and poppies, which were rendered in the soft, natural colors then available in Berlin wools. The replacement of these by the harder, more strident colors of the chemically produced (from coal tar) aniline dyes coincided with the development of greenhouse culture. Gaily colored annuals and showy exotics joined the old favorites, which had also become overblown and blowsy by being forced in hothouses rather than grown in gardens. An ideal bed, according to Mrs. Loudon, was one "so brilliant with bright scarlet verbenas and golden yellow calceolarias that one can scarcely gaze at it in the sunshine." When, in the 1870s, carpet bedding gave way to "leaf embroidery," the shades used in what was to be the last phase of Berlin woolwork became correspondingly more muted. Leaf embroidery used only foliage plants or plants such as geraniums whose flowers could be picked off.

In the garden, as in needlework, the brilliance of the flowers was intensified by the contrast of a dark, even background. Thanks to Thomas Budding's invention of a revolutionary new mowing machine, lawns could now be clipped smooth, or made "velvety," at little cost and with relatively little effort. A scythe was difficult to wield, and in order to keep the blade sharp, it was first necessary to flatten the ground by rolling it. It was the combination of lawns and flower beds which excited Molly, heroine of Mrs. Gaskell's novel *Wives and Daughters* (1866), when she visited her neighbors at The Towers: "green velvet lawns, bathed in sunshine . . . and flower beds too, scarlet, crimson, blue and orange; masses of blossom lying on the greensward." Velvet lawns were no less appealing in the United States. "The velvety lawn, flecked with sunlight and the shadows of common trees," wrote Frank J. Scott in 1870, "[is an] inexpensive, and may be a very elegant refreshment for the business-wearied eye." Scott, a landscape architect, thought that the garden planner should think of the lawn as a lady's gown of green velvet and of the flower beds as bits of lace or decoration.

On the new, close-cut lawns people sat in deck chairs, played croquet, took tea, and held garden parties. The charmed silences of the garden, wrote the architect John Sedding late in the century, were broken by "the healthy interests of common daily life—the romps of children, the clink of tea-cups, [and] the clatter of croquet-mallets." Enter the modern lawn.

## NOSTALGIA FOR

## THE COUNTRYSIDE

The return of flowers to the garden and the interest taken in even a mechanical form of embroidery are now seen as symptoms of a widespread desire for country things. Victorians clamored for writings about nature and the countryside. Isaac Walton's *Compleat Angler* (1653) and Gilbert White's *Natural History of Selborne* (1789) were best-sellers. As in earlier times, the nostalgia for things rural drew much of its strength from dissatisfaction with urban life. But what had been mere murmurings in the eighteenth century swelled, in the nineteenth, to a chorus of complaint. By 1800, towns and cities housed one-quarter of the British population, and by 1851 more than half.

Deterioration of the urban environment, already discernible in some of the larger English cities in the sixteenth and seventeenth centuries, had reached an advanced stage by the nineteenth. Sulphurous smoke darkened the air, dirtied clothes, ruined draperies, and killed flowers and trees. Visitors to Sheffield, as to all sizeable industrial cities, expected to be "choked" with smoke. Equally foul were the pollutants generated by brewing, dyeing, starch making, and brick manufacture, all of which were carried on in the center of the nineteenth century city. "Immers'd in smoke [and] stunn'd with perpetual noise," town dwellers yearned for greenery and the imagined delights of rural life. "Man immured in cities," as Cowper had put it in 1785, still retained an "inextinguishable thirst for rural scenes," and when denied them, he was forced to "compensate the loss by supplemental shifts, the best he may." The instinct for the country, Cowper maintained, was "inborn":

> And they that never pass their brick-wall bounds
> To range the fields and treat their lungs with air
> Yet feel the burning instinct; over-head
> Suspend their crazy boxes, planted thick,
> And watered duly. There the pitcher stands
> A fragment, and the spoutless teapot there;
> Sad witnesses how close-pent man regrets
> The country, with what order he contrives
> A peep at nature, when he can no more.

# Nineteenth-Century Villas

In some cases he contrived more than a peep. Readers of Dickens' *Little Dorrit* (1855–57) may remember Mrs. Plornish's shop parlor, one wall of which had been painted to resemble the exterior of a thatched cottage. Hollyhocks and sunflowers grew beside the walls, dense smoke issued from the chimney, a faithful dog guarded the threshold, and a cloud of pigeons rose from a circular pigeon house behind the garden paling. On the door, which pipe-smoking Mr. Plornish had a habit of leaning against after work, was a brass plate inscribed "Happy Cottage, T. and M. Plornish." It made no difference to Mrs. Plornish that Mr. Plornish's eye was some inches above the level of the gable bedroom in the thatch and that his hands uprooted the blooming garden; she rejoiced "unspeakably" in the deception. To come out into the shop after it was closed, and hear her father sing a song inside this cottage, was "a perfect Pastoral to Mrs. Plornish, the Golden Age revived." In the Plornish household, *rus* had been firmly implanted in *urbe*.

With no shop to hold him and with money to spare, Dickens had no need of a fantasy or "Cockney cottage." He assuaged his own longing for the countryside by getting out of the city. At his country home in Gad's Hill, Kent, he worked in a summer house—an imitation Swiss chalet—in which five carefully placed mirrors reflected and refracted the scene outdoors: leaves quivering at the windows, great fields of waving corn, and the sail-dotted river. "My room," he wrote, "is up among the branches of the trees; and the birds and the butterflies fly in and out, and the green branches shoot in, at the open windows, and the lights and shadows of the clouds come and go with the rest of the company. The scent of the flowers, and indeed of every thing that is growing for miles and miles, is most delicious."

Few nineteenth-century writers failed to comment on the townspeople's loss of the countryside. "Where all is stone around, blank wall and hot pavement," wrote Charlotte Bronte in 1853, "how precious seems one shrub, how lovely an enclosed and planted spot of ground." Hazlitt, in his essay "On the Love of the Country" (1814), wrote of the nostalgic hold of rural objects on displaced country people, and in particular of the power of trees, flowers, and animals to bring back memories of childhood. Yet the transition from a rural to an urban-industrial society was seen not just as the painful exchange of an attractive for an ugly setting. It was also regarded, as Raymond Williams pointed out, as a kind of fall, the true cause and origin of social suffering and disorder. Conditions for the laboring poor were, if anything, worse in the country than in the towns, but the myth of a nurturing rural society had a powerful influence on social thought. It was taken for granted that true communities could be found only in the countryside. There dwelt, in the imagination of the town dweller, a "natural order," a hierarchy that was stable, virtuous, and paternalistic. A young Victorian needleworker, who evidently saw herself as a protector and preserver of Old English values, fixed the perception in a verse that she appended to an embroidered landscape:

> Will my dearest papa accept from my hand,
> A trifling estate and freehold, the land
> The buildings I raised; I planted the trees
> The waters I formed for convenience and ease:
> The castle looks well, and will stand many years
> A pleasant retreat for you and your heirs,
> When with business fatigued, or sick of the town,
> The boat may attend to waft you safe down
> The servants are humble, neat, cleanly, and still,
> No impertinent answers disputing your will.

Despite its falsities, Victorian sentiment for country things reflected an authentic longing that increased both in volume and intensity as cities spread and industries grew. At the Great Exhibition of 1851, naturalism dominated every branch of decorative art. Carpets so "rifled" the flower garden of its gayest and choicest flowers that, as one observer noted, only those well-versed in botany could identify their contents. Critics of design complained bitterly of an "objectionable" degree of naturalism: of carpets "ornamented with lilies on their natural bed" and of "palm trees and landscapes . . . used as the ornaments of muslin curtains." The taste persisted late into the century. In 1879 a critic voiced his objections: "One may approach the hostess over a carpet strewn with bouquets, converse with one foot upon a Bengal tiger, and contemplate birds of Paradise upon the wall. . . . Do we not everywhere find flowers upon floor carpets, fruit upon dessert plates, insects and birds upon the walls?"

**WILLIAM MORRIS**     The age's most celebrated exponent of the natural, and, by extension, its most determined enemy of mechanistic urban industrialism, was the English poet, craftsman, and socialist William Morris (b. 1834; d. 1896). But instead of following the general taste for the exotic, Morris turned to that most unadulterated of English settings: the fields and gardens of the Middle Ages. He often pleased himself, he once wrote, "with trying to realize the face of medieval England; the many chases and great woods, the stretches of common tillage and common pasture quite unenclosed; the rough husbandry of the tilled parts, the unimproved breeds of cattle, sheep, and swine . . . the strings of packhorses along the bridle roads . . . the villages . . . better and more populous; their churches . . . all crowded with altars and furniture, and gay with pictures and ornament."

He laid out the garden of Red House, the home he built in an orchard in Kent, along the lines of a medieval pleasance: four small square gardens each surrounded by a rose-covered wattle fence. Mackail, his first biographer, wrote of a garden with long grass walks, midsummer lilies, autumn sunflowers, and wattled rose trellises enclosing richly flowered square garden plots. Morris's ideal was a walled garden divided by "old clipped yew hedges" and flower beds boxed in a way that made the garden seem, if not part of the house, then "at least the clothes of it." He thought that clothing the house ought to be the aim of garden design. Carpet bedding he regarded as "an aberration of the human mind," the very thought of which could make him "blush with shame," even when quite alone. He was no fonder of the "florist" plants, bred for size, color, and scent, with which the beds were filled. Subtlety of form, delicacy of texture, and sweetness of color had all been sacrificed. Even the rose, "the flower of flowers," had suffered. Morris's pet hatreds were the scarlet geranium and the yellow calceolaria, frequently grown together in order, he supposed, "to show that even flowers can be thoroughly ugly."

When Morris began to decorate Red House, nothing that was ready-made appealed, so he designed what he needed himself. He hung the walls of the principal bedroom with simple indigo-dyed blue serge that his wife Jane embroidered with red, white, and yellow flowers, spacing them as if they were in a flowery mead. The hanging, which became the model for the wallpaper "Daisy," was Morris's first attempt at making "unmistakable suggestions of gardens and fields." The effect, as he described it, was to "turn [their] chamber walls into the green woods of the leafy month of June, populous of bird and beast." Embroidery once again had brought the garden indoors, and with it, as Thomasina Beck remarked, came echoes of a far-off world of romance and chivalry.

Though renowned for his wallpapers, Morris regarded them as a poor substitute for tapestries and printed hangings. His response to tapestry was truly medieval: "Well I remember as a boy my first acquaintance with a room hung with faded greenery . . . in Epping Forest . . . and the impression of romance it made upon me! a feeling that always comes back to me when I read . . . the description of the Green Room at Monkbarns, amongst which the novelist [Sir Walter Scott] has with such exquisite cunning of art imbedded the fresh and glittering verses of the summer poet Chaucer: yes, that was more than upholstery, believe me."

When decorating large houses, Morris's usual practice was to use oak wainscotting for the lower walls and tapestry above. By fashioning plane upon plane of rich, crisp, and varying foliage with bright blossoms and

*The Woodpecker*, William Morris, 1885. Tapestries such as these turned walls into hedges and forests. (The William Morris Gallery, Walthamstow, London)

# Nineteenth-Century Villas

strange birds showing through the intervals, one may, he once remarked, "almost turn [one's] wall into a rose hedge or a deep forest." True scale, perspective, and the aerial effects of Renaissance design he condemned as "wholly unfit for tapestry."

Displeased with the colors of chemical dyes, which he found either muddy or loud, Morris turned to older practices. From herbals acquired in England and France he learned how to make vegetable dyes of clear, unfading color. "I was at Kelmscott the other day, and betwixt the fishing, I cut a handful of poplar twigs and boiled them, and dyed a lock of wool a very good yellow." As well as adding to his store of conventions for representing natural forms, the bold woodcuts of the herbals also taught him the value of definite form and firm outlines.

Morris's objectives in decoration were social as well as aesthetic. By insisting that his works be handmade, he could serve only the affluent, but his aim was reform: nothing less, he once wrote, than to dispel "the prevailing darkness of ugliness that ha[d] covered all modern life." An essay or a lecture by Morris was never a narrow discourse on his art or—as he preferred to call it—his craft. Design mattered only if it improved everyday life and contributed to human happiness. Art's domain was the whole human environment, and it ought therefore to touch "every one of the things that goes to make up the surroundings" among which people live.

As defined by Morris, art embraced town planning as well as the design and decoration of individual buildings. He was an ardent promoter of new towns and model communities. His desire to turn Britain "from the grimy backyard of a workshop into a garden" and his notion of a balance between town and countryside anticipated the "garden city" movement. "I want the town to be impregnated with the country, and the country with the intelligence and vivid life of the town . . . I want every homestead to be . . . a lovely house surrounded by acres and acres of garden . . . I want the town to be in short, a garden with beautiful houses in it." For Morris, the question of suitable surroundings was "the most serious . . . a man can think of; for [it was] no less than the chances of a calm, dignified, and therefore happy life for the mass of mankind."

In the poorer districts of cities he deplored the practice of building houses and streets unadorned by gardens or parks. And in new housing estates in the richer districts he thought buildings should be fitted around existing trees instead of—the usual practice—clearing the site until it was as bare as the pavement. Without trees urban life was intolerable: "One trembles at the very sound of an axe as one sits at one's work at home." Morris practiced what he preached. The building of Red House was so carefully planned that hardly a tree in the cherry and apple orchard had to be cut down; "apples fell in at the windows as they stood open on hot autumn nights." And at Merton Abbey one of his first changes was to plant poplars, which are quick growing, about the wooden work sheds of the old silk mill. Flowers were planted too, and with the trees they soon gave the place a garden air for which it became famous.

Morris realized, however, that people starved for natural beauty would in most cases have to settle for simulations of it in wallpapers, rugs, and chintzes. Without broadcasting its presence, an imaginative wall covering could, he once remarked, turn a room into a bower or refuge. Like nature itself, the simulations would both "soothe and elevate." Morris, who subscribed to the then widely held belief that surroundings influenced mood and behavior, was an environmentalist in the Andrew Jackson Downing mold. He thought that carelessly decorated walls could drive people to unrest or callousness, but walls that were a "visible symbol" of nature, that showed "the outward face of the earth . . . the innocent love of animals, or . . . man passing his days between work and rest" could only be soothing. The desire to turn rooms into gardens and whole houses into pleasances lay behind all his papers and textiles. The ideal was "a dwelling that does not lack the beauty which nature would freely allow it, if [people's] own perversity did not turn nature out of doors." On going into the main rooms at Kelmscott House, Bruce Glasier felt "a delightful sense of garden-like freshness and bloom."

Committed to naturalism, Morris rejected the abstract, geometric patterns then being promoted by rival designers. All materials required that plants and animals be represented by conventions, but he believed that only in the coarsest were symbols necessary. As "a Western man," and a lover of pictures, not symbols, he insisted on overt meaning in his patterns: "I must have unmistakable suggestions of gardens and fields, and strange trees, boughs and tendrils." More, he wanted a sense of growth, "strong and crisp," in the vegetal elements of all patterns. "Take heed . . . that the lines do not get thready or flabby or too far from their stock to sprout firmly and vigorously; even where a line ends it should look as if it had plenty of capacity for more growth if so it would."

The richness and suggestiveness of Morris's designs were a mark of his receptivity to nature. He loved plants. Mackail quotes a series of passages from letters any one of which might have been a program for a tapestry or a wallpaper: "The fields are all butter-cuppy. The elms are mostly green up to their tops: the hawthorn not out but the crabs beautiful, and also that whitebeam (I think they call it) with the umbelliferous flowers. In the garden we have lots of tulips out looking beautiful; the white bluebells and some blue ones; some of the anemones are in blossom and they all soon will be: they are

"Unmistakable suggestions of gardens and fields": a bed hanging at Kelmscott made by William Morris's daughter, May Morris. (Courtesy, Royal Commission on the Historical Monuments of England)

very lovely." And: "Blue cornflowers and red poppies, growing together with the corn round the roots of the fruit trees, in their shadows, and sweeping up to the brows of the long, low hills till they reached the sky, changing sometimes into long fields of vines, or delicate, lush green forage."

In later life, Morris emphasized the need for simplicity in decoration. He thought that congested living rooms ought to be cleared of their "farrago of rubbish" and replaced by objects that are "natural and reasonable." In private he would often wave aside his own work, declaring that he would prefer "a sanded floor and whitewashed walls, and the green trees and flowering meads and living waters outside." By anticipating the end of ornament and the birth of functionalism, he was one of the earliest heralds of the modern movement. This he could do, as Paul Foot remarked, because his aims were social and his art directed always at society's needs.

**SCENIC**

**WALLPAPER**

While the young William Morris had eyes only for a distant past, most of his contemporaries hungered for glimpses of distant places. No age was more curious of geography. Expanding European empires, near-universal literacy, travelers' tales, and illustrated books and magazines whetted appetites for news and views of distant or foreign parts. Thomas Cook opened his travel bureau in 1845, but his services were beyond the means of most people. The combination of readily available information and restricted movement created an appetite for vicarious experience. If people were unable to travel to distant places, then might not distant places be brought to them?

The problem of representing landscapes more comprehensive than could be taken in from a single point of view had engaged painters, inventors, and optical scientists for more than a century. Painters of conventional panoramas circumvented the problem by taking imaginary vantage points high above the scene to be painted; but the view, though far more extensive than the one at ground level, was still limited. Carmontelle, the inventive eighteenth-century French playwright, architect, and landscape gardener, reached a partial solution by unrolling, in an optical viewer, a translucent frieze on which a continuous landscape had been painted. As the rollers turned, the scene passed in front of the stationary spectator. Carmontelle's device was an elaboration of earlier experiments in which painted glass, angled mirrors, and turntables had been used to create the illusion of an unfolding landscape.

Not until the end of the eighteenth century, however, was a satisfactory solution found to the problem of displaying landscape panoramas on a large scale to large numbers of people. In the 1780s Robert Barker painted the entire city of Edinburgh, as seen from Carlton Hill, as a continuous landscape on the interior walls of a large circular building. Barker patented the painting in 1787 and exhibited it in London as well as in Edinburgh. Within a decade or two, people in every major city were paying to enter rotundas (variously named panoramas, dioramas, or cosmoramas) where they might see the re-creation of a major battle, a view of a famed landscape or city landscape, or the natives and countryside of some exotic land. In 1801 an Ameri-

# Nineteenth-Century Villas

can opened two rotundas near the boulevard Montmartre in Paris; one showed the city of Paris, the other the siege of Toulon. "Panorama painting," wrote the English painter John Constable in 1803, "seems all the rage." He pointed out that it was remarkable for sheer spectacle rather than artistic merit, yet from time to time panorama painting attracted distinguished painters. Thomas Girtin made an enormous panorama of London—the *Eidometropolis*—and Hendrik Mesdag an equally large one of Schevening that can still be seen in a building in the Hague especially designed for its display.

Visitors to London's Vauxhall Gardens in the 1820s and 1830s might have seen panoramas of the Bay of Naples by moonlight, including "a Vivid Representation of Vesuvius in a State of Active Combustion"; or Mont Blanc and the valley of the Chamouni by moonlight; Venice from the Adriatic; an "Immense" scenic representation of the Balkan Pass; or the whole of the polar scenery. In the 1860s Berlin alone had six panoramas. The paintings were lit from above and viewed from a roofed platform in the center of the hall. The only light to reach the spectators was that reflected from the surface of the painting; and to make it appear more brilliant, passages and stairways leading to the platform were kept nearly dark.

Though the sense of being in the center of a brilliantly lighted landscape required special settings and equipment, similar effects could be achieved in the house. Roll window blinds, painted with a landscape or cityscape "in the brightest transparent tints," produced the effect of a translucent frieze. When lowered, the blind was illuminated by the daylight behind it. Surviving examples of American translucent window blinds from the 1830s and 1840s suggest that landscapes were the most popular designs. In 1844 the New York Transparent Window Shade Manufacturing Company advertised "fancy sketches, moonlight views, Gothic landscape centers, [and] Tintern Abbeys." Downing condemned the views as "vulgar," but he grudgingly allowed that in towns and cities they did serve to "awaken a sentiment of nature in the midst of brick walls."

The sense of enveloping space, created by the panoramas, could also be simulated by painting or, more commonly in the nineteenth century, by pasting images onto walls. The first European landscape papers were similar in conception to paintings. John Jackson of Battersea, for example, made panels of papers, framed by paper borders, designed to fit the spaces of particular rooms. He offered landscapes after Salvator Rosa and Claude Lorraine, views of Venice after Canaletto, and copies of all the best painters of the Italian, French, and Flemish schools. In 1774 the colonial governor of New Jersey, William Franklin, commissioned a New York City importer to obtain wallpaper for a house he was to occupy. The papers were to be made "on Purpose to suit the Pannels, Chimney, etc." and were to be stained or painted with the falls of Passaic, Cohoes, and Niagara.

Early in the nineteenth century, wallpapers appeared which used all four walls, save where they were interrupted by windows and doors, to create a continuous, non-repeating panorama. They depended on a method of printing, developed in France, which made it possible to join together separate sheets to form a continuous pattern or image. Scenic wallpapers, or "scenics," as they came to be known in the trade, were a novelty in decoration. Frescoes and tapestries may have filled walls with gardens and landscapes, but the space represented was seldom continuous or encircling. Chinese wallpapers, with their continuous, non-repeating patterns, were obvious antecedents of the French scenics, but their generally flat patterns seldom created the the same sense of environing space.

So absorbing were the scenics that, when first produced, they were the rage of continental Europe and the United States. Their enthusiastic transatlantic reception Phyllis Ackerman, a historian of wallpaper, ascribed to the serious limitations of life in the young republic. One of these was simply an inability to make enough wallpaper of any kind; the scarcity of old rags, one observer noted, made paper "excessively dear." When Brissot de Warville visited the United States in 1788, he declared that wallpaper was the one article of commerce for which Europeans need not fear a reciprocal competition. But the particular attractions of landscape papers in the United States had nothing to do with scarcity of materials. Diversions in the republic were simple and few, and it was isolated from the rest of the world. Travel for pleasure was almost out of the question. Journeys between cities could take days and an Atlantic voyage a month to six weeks under trying and sometimes dangerous conditions. Vicarious experience, too, was more difficult to come by than in Europe. Books, circulating libraries, and even magazines were less readily available. Illustrated wallpapers, therefore, filled horizons that might otherwise have been empty.

The wallpapers were arranged in sets of small sheets, and—if oceans had to be crossed—they were sometimes wrapped in tin foil tubes to protect them from damp sea air. Though perishable, the papers were easily transported and could be bought in most large U.S. cities soon after their release in France. The sheets were numbered, and when the sets reached their destination, they were pieced together on walls by the aid of charts not unlike those used in children's picture puzzles. A complete set, of between twenty and thirty strips, was sufficient to cover the walls of a fair-sized room between wainscot or chair rail and ceiling. The strips, about 20 inches wide and between 8 and 10 feet long, had generous expanses of sky so that they

# Nineteenth-Century Villas

could be cut to fit walls of varying heights without damage to the more densely decorated parts of the paper.

To the austere houses of early American colonists, the papers brought, as historian Nancy McClelland put it, "a riot of colour that appeared almost licentious after the severity of whitewashed walls. They filled the rooms with movement, with romance, and with light . . . [giving] the exact note of abandon needed to redeem the asperity and bareness of these colonial interiors."* After visiting a house in New York City in 1891, George Alfred Townsend made note of "the foreign wall-paper, in large landscapes, [which represented] hunters on horseback with guns and dogs breaking into Rhenish vales where milkmaids are surprised and invite flirtations. The human figures [were] nearly a foot high; the mountains and woods, rocks and streams, panoramic; the colors, daring and loud." He liked the paper because it was "Dutchy" and because it would have taken Martin Van Buren, who had hung it, "into the atmosphere of Jordaens and Van der Halst." Though restricted at first to the houses of the wealthy, scenic wallpapers could, by the middle of the nineteenth century, be found in the homes of prosperous merchants, businessmen, and professionals across the country. A set was found recently in a modest house in California where, during the nineteenth century, it had been pasted directly onto the interior wooden partitions. A two-story frame house, offered for sale in Brooklyn in 1835, had landscape wallpapers in entrance and stair halls, the parlor, and sitting and drawing rooms. Houses then had fewer furnishings than houses today, and entrance halls and dining and billiard rooms, in particular, were virtually bare. Scenics prominently displayed just inside the doorway of the house made such a grand impression that in American newspapers and magazines they were sometimes advertised as "well calculated for Halls and Passages."

Scenics were also popular in public places. The English writer Harriet Martineau noted, in *Retrospective of Western Travels* (1838), that hotel parlors in various parts of the country were covered with "old-fashioned papers," which she believed to be French. They showed panoramas of hunting parties, fleets of ships, or other such diversified scenes. At Schenectady, the Bay of Naples, with its fishing boats on the water and groups of lazzaroni [idlers] on the shore, "adorned [the] parlor walls." In public rooms, the papers were far from objects of veneration despite subjects that were often classical or decorously rural. Irreverent Americans reduced the scenics to comic strips

---

*Early settlers in Puritan New England were forced to restrain a love of color and got into trouble when they tried to satisfy it. In 1639 the Reverend Thomas Allen of Charlestown, Massachusetts, was summoned before a court for allegedly painting his house a lively color. He escaped reprimand only by proving that the culprit was the previous owner.

by putting speeches into the mouths of the figures. American witticisms issuing, in the now-familiar balloons, from the mouths of Neapolitan fishermen struck Harriet Martineau as distinctly odd. But defacement may well have been the fate of all publicly displayed scenics. When Balzac, in *Père Goriot* (1834), described the dining room of a dingy Parisian boarding house, he referred to "un papier verni," a varnished wallpaper, which a succession of lodgers had made the subject of ribald jokes.

Most of the scenic papers came from France, which, as a friend of the Revolution and an ally in the 1812 war against Britain, enjoyed exceptionally warm relations with the United States. Scenics were not popular in England. An Englishman from Bath, visiting France in 1802, found Parisian wallpaper so "vulgar" that after returning home he relined his walls with satin. Later in the century the architect-designer Augustus Pugin, one of the czars of taste in nineteenth-century England, pronounced that wallpaper should remain true to its two-dimensional character and not imitate other forms of decoration. In deference to Pugin, English walls remained unashamedly flat, their strict architectural function unsullied by pictures that created an illusion of distance or depth.

Well-to-do Americans, on the other hand, were more than willing to forsake the sanctity of their walls for the pleasures of being transported to the tourist meccas of Europe or other exotic corners of the world. Country people thrilled to the sight of foreign cities, and harried city dwellers were calmed by pictures of serene countrysides and gardens. French papers were a consistent presidential favorite. John Quincy Adams ordered a set of Joseph Dufour's "Vues de Italie," Andrew Jackson chose "Telemachus in the Island of Calypso" for the hall of the Hermitage, near Nashville, Tennessee, and Martin Van Buren bought Jean Zuber's "Landscape of the Hunt" for the hall of his house in Kinderhook, New York. Even newborn Americans took pleasure in the scenics. "I was born," Kate Sanborn wrote delightedly at the beginning of this century, "at the foot of Mount Vesuvius and there was a merry dance to the music of mandolin and tambourine round the tomb of Vergil on my natal morn. Some men were fishing, others bringing in the catch; further on was a picnic party, sentimental youths and maidens eating comfits and dainties to the tender note of a flute; and old Vesuvius smoking violently. All this because the room in which I made my debut was adorned with a landscape, or scenic wallpaper."

The geographical range of the French papers, and something of their character, can be elicited from the advertising. Newspapers in almost every city of any size carried detailed advertisements for "Views" and "Long Strip Landscapes." William Mooney of New York City offered, in 1802, a set "representing one of the most enchanting landscapes which can be imagined all in

# Nineteenth-Century Villas

the most natural colors agreeable to nature, from the stone on the river's bank to the golden tinged cloud in the air." In 1817 James H. Foster of Boston offered: RICH PAPER HANGINGS JUST RECEIVED: Setts of Monuments of Paris, a very elegant hanging. Setts of the River Bosphorus. Do. English Gardens. Capt. Cook's Voyage. Do. . . . Views of Switzerland—Hindostan Scenery. Do. . . . Views in Italy—Water scenes. Views in Turkey—Roman Scenery. Do. Ports of Bordeaux and Bayonne, Elysian Fields, Grecian Arcadia, and many other landscape papers, making as great a variety as can be found at any store in town." A Boston competitor, J. Bumstead and Son, offered "ELEGANT FRENCH PAPER HANGINGS," among which were "4 sets of Views, representing a Tiger Hunt—Hunting the Deer—Fishing—and Chinese Scenes with Borders."

Wallpaper manufacturers also catered to literary and historical tastes. Often they were able to combine these with the taste for travel. The adventures of Robinson Crusoe and Don Quixote were illustrated, as were the conquests of Pizarro and the voyages of Captain Cook. Other popular subjects with geographical connotations were journeys and voyages from myth and legend, and military campaigns. Taking their cue from French war artists, wallpaper designers began to illustrate the most famous passages of arms in the Napoleonic oeuvre. The thirty six sheets of the *Battle of Austerlitz* (1814) recounted the famous victory over the emperors of Russia and Austria. Other papers celebrated Napoleon's campaign in Egypt and the daily life of the French soldier. Nor were American victories neglected: In 1838 the Zuber Company of Alsace brought out the *War of American Independence*. For observers the viewing was made easy. Most papers, figuratively speaking, were in large print: The figures were often 1 to 2 feet high, and a single scene could fill an entire wall.

Except for battle scenes, where topographical accuracy mattered, the papers presented typical rather than actual landscapes. Typical landscapes were composites, made of the features thought to be characteristic of particular places or environments. City as well as country landscapes were generalized. In city scenes the designers used actual buildings and monuments, but to fit them into the available space, they were forced to make neighbors of buildings that were miles apart. To make *Monuments of Paris* (1815) and *Views of London* (ca. 1830s/1840s), Joseph Dufour, for example, removed prominent buildings from their settings and lined them up along the banks of the Seine and the Thames. Sometimes entire cities were moved. In Pignet and Paillard's *Paris-Rome-Londres* (1852) the cities were grouped around an adjoining hill.

Generalized landscapes were even more footloose. Two of Jean Zuber's most popular papers, *Isola Bella* (1844) and *Eldorado* (1848), had only token

*Savages of the Pacific Ocean* or *The Voyages of Captain Cook*, panels 11–20, Joseph Dufour, ca. 1806. Scenic wallpapers were undisguisedly didactic. Dufour's came with a printed brochure that described the places and events depicted in each of the panels. On the far left are inhabitants of New Zealand and on the far right inhabitants of the Pelow islands, in the western Pacific. (The Fine Arts Museums of San Francisco, gift of Georgia M. Worthington and The Fine Arts Museums Trustees Fund)

connections with particular places. Each is dominated by a fringe of luxuriant tropical or subtropical plants representing the vegetation of equatorial Brazil and the north Italian lakes. In 1855, two years after Zuber's death, the Zuber Company issued a thirty-one-sheet set of a polar seascape, the first of a projected series of papers (*Zones of the Earth*) designed to show the range of natural environments between the polar regions and the tropics. The idea for the series (which was never completed) may well have been sown by Alexander von Humboldt. Humboldt was a persistent advocate of paintings and panoramas as a means of raising, as he phrased it, the feeling of admiration for nature. In the second volume of *Cosmos* (1847), he urged that rotundas be built in large cities specifically for the display of panoramas illustrating the vegetation of particular geographical latitudes and particular zones of elevation. Humboldt's aspiration was consistent with the scientific spirit of eighteenth-century exploration. Its exemplars were James Cook and Joseph Banks and its chief beneficiaries botanists and horticulturists.

*Monuments of Paris*, Joseph Dufour, 1814. In his city landscapes, Dufour often removed prominent buildings from their settings and lined them up along the banks of a river, in this case the Seine. (Courtesy, The Henry Francis du Pont Winterthur Museum. Bequest of Henry Francis duPont, 1969)

So great was the public demand for information that wallpaper manufacturers made no effort to disguise the didactic purposes of their papers. Theophile Gautier could remark wryly that the walls of a dining room in a Simplon inn were "an encyclopaedia worth consulting while waiting for the soup," but more earnest nineteenth-century diners would have prized decorations that instructed as well as entertained. A lengthy exegesis usually accompanied each set of scenics. Historical incidents were explained, fre-

*Eldorado*, Jean Zuber, 1848. A typical or generalized rain forest landscape that represented the vegetation of equatorial Brazil. Zuber's objective, which he never realized, was to illustrate each of the major natural environments between the poles and the equator. (By courtesy of the Board of Trustees of the Victoria & Albert Museum)

# Nineteenth-Century Villas

quently in what we would now regard as tiresome detail, and advice given about the most advantageous arrangement of the strips. In some sets, pieces were designed especially for use in the narrow spaces between windows and above doors.

In the booklet made to accompany the Captain Cook papers, but distributed well before the papers were ready for sale, Joseph Dufour owned to having been motivated by lofty educational objectives. By offering the papers, Dufour hoped not only to acquaint the public with new lands and peoples, but also to create "a community of taste and enjoyment" between people who lived in a state of civilization and those who were "at the outset of their native intelligence." A cultivated man familiar with the history of exploration and the accounts of travelers might, "without even leaving his room, [have found] himself in the presence of these people, and see[n] their lives unfold around him." Mothers, charged with the all-important task of molding the minds of the young, would find that the set afforded "an immense curriculum of things to teach children." Daughters (the boys were taught at school) could get "living" lessons in geography and history, and by studying the trees and plants, they would be introduced to botany. These objectives now seem naively high-minded, but Dufour knew his audience. He was merely capitalizing on the general reverence for learning and on the widely held belief, laid down by John Ruskin in England and Andrew Jackson Downing in the United States, that surroundings ought to be instructive and improving as well as pleasant. Moral principles, both men affirmed, lay behind aesthetic choices.

Despite the scarcity of rags, Americans began producing their own scenic papers early in the century. Anxious to see improvements in the design of American papers, Moses Grant of Boston offered for sale, in 1813, "fashionable Hangings for Rooms" which were intended to obviate "the objection of too much sameness, by introducing a variety of views." Design, paper, colors, and labor were, he emphasized, "all American and [bore] the closest comparison with imported papers. Jean Zuber responded by offering *North American Views* (1834). The views were popular tourist attractions: West Point on the Hudson River, New York Bay, Boston Harbor, Niagara Falls, the Natural Bridge of Virginia, and a dance of the Winnebago Indians. A set, removed from a house in Maryland, now hangs in the oval-shaped diplomatic reception room at the White House.

So costly was the process of making scenic wallpapers that even the successful French manufacturers were constantly on the alert for economies. A set of papers could take years to design and plan, and each issue was the subject of an international sales promotion. The scenes were built up from the impressions of hundreds, or even thousands, of engraved woodblocks.

*Monuments of Paris*, for example, required 2,062 separate blocks. For colored papers, series of blocks had to be cut for each part of the design. The first block was for the outline, subsequent ones for each of the colors in the design; in *Monuments of Paris* eighty colors were used.

To reduce costs, papers were sometimes produced in monochrome rather than full color. Shades of gray—*en grisaille*—and brown—*en bistre, en chocolat*, or *en nanquin*—were particularly popular. But to recoup the huge outlay, even the most cheaply produced paper had to sell over many years. To accommodate changes in taste and circumstance, papers were edited, like books. In 1838 Zuber added hand-painted figures, engaged in battle, to his *North American Views* and reissued it as the *War of American Independence*. In American battle scenes topographical accuracy seems not to have been important.

## AMERICAN

## WALL PAINTINGS

Even with production economies, scenic papers were a luxury well beyond the means of most American householders. It also took an expert to hang them, and, needing height, they could not be fitted into the low-ceilinged rooms of many rural houses. In any case, they could be bought only in cities. For country people, in particular, the least expensive alternative was to substitute a painted landscape for a printed one. Someone with a brush, some artistic sense, a few rolls of paper, and some tempera colors could accomplish in a few weeks, or even less, what would take a dozen wood engravers a year. The results, inevitably, were rougher. Usually no outlines were drawn, and the colors were applied impressionistically with broad sweeps of the brush.

If tacked rather than pasted onto the walls, painted papers could be taken down if the household moved. But if moveability was not a consideration, decorators in North America frequently resorted to wall paintings. In rural areas itinerant painters, in exchange for bed and board and a small fee, would rapidly decorate a parlor, a bedroom, or a public meeting room. For standard features they used stencils stiffened with oil and paint; the rest they painted freehand. Dry pigments mixed with glue or egg white and water to produce the substance known as tempera were applied directly to the dry plaster wall. Tempera—a fast-drying medium—required painters to work quickly and surely.

The painters were members of the colorful fellowship of Yankee peddlers, which included doctors, lawyers, preachers, teachers, and puppeteers, who took to every outpost the latest gifts of civilization. Traveling on foot and horseback, or by stagecoach and canal boat, and carrying carpetbags, saddlebags, or small wooden trunks covered with deer hide or pigskin, they

# Nineteenth-Century Villas

ranged along the eastern seaboard and through New England, upstate New York, and Ohio, offering to make walls "right smart and pretty." The best known of the peddler-painters was Rufus Porter, an inventor and promoter as well as a house and sign painter, who worked out simple techniques for painting murals. Between 1825 and 1845 he and his pupils and assistants are thought to have painted landscapes on the walls of several hundred New England houses.

As well as being a skilled and prolific practitioner, Porter was a great promoter of wall painting. One of his boasts was that given a "competent supply" of painters, he could virtually eliminate the need for wall hangings. Wallpaper he seems to have deplored. Not only was it "apt to be torn off" but it was also a veritable breeding ground "for various kinds of insects." He began his advocacy of wall painting with an entry in a small but very popular book, *A Select Collection of Valuable and Curious Arts and Interesting Experiments* (1825). Among the "curious arts" were recipes for changing the color of horses and helpful hints for kindling a fire underwater. The instructions on wall painting he later amplified into articles for the *New York Mechanic* and *Scientific American*, both of which magazines he published and edited.

In the interests of speed and economy, Porter advised that some of the painting be done mechanically. Buildings could be rendered with stencils and more complex objects, such as steamboats and trains, with transfers. Foliage could be stamped on with a cork bottle stopper or stippled with a brush. An artist skilled in these techniques could, Porter maintained in an April 1846 issue of the *Scientific American*, paint an entire room in a matter of hours: "We have seen an artist in this branch paint the entire walls of a parlor, with all the several distances, and a variety of fancy scenery, palaces, villages, mills, vessels etc., and a beautiful set of shade trees on the foreground, and finish the same complete in less than five hours." To prop up the ceilings of rooms whose walls, figuratively speaking, had been removed by landscape paintings, Porter was in the habit of painting tall foreground trees.

Like all itinerant painters, Porter was able to offer two kinds of scenery: "from nature" and "fancy." Scenery from nature was the familiar American, or New England, countryside, whereas that from fancy was of places distant in time or space. Fancy scenes might have been abstracted from landscapes on imported wallpapers, pictures in illustrated magazines, or copies of old masters. Sometimes, to please their clients, itinerant painters mixed plain and fancy by introducing ruins, volcanoes, and palm trees into—usually stylized—American scenes.

The itinerants seldom tackled actual views. New England scenes were composites, conceived in the mind's eye, of features thought to be typical of

Wall paintings by Rufus Porter in the Patricia Holsaert house, Hancock, New Hampshire. The paintings, "from nature," show substantial houses and productive farmland; they are reassuring. (Photograph courtesy Whitney Museum of American Art, The Flowering of American Folk Art: 1776–1876 by Jean Lipman and Alice Winchester)

the district or region. The scenes were invariably cheerful: thriving villages and towns, prosperous farmlands, and busy harbors, all painted with bold brush strokes in bright, primary colors. Porter was an enthusiast of the American scene long before it was fashionable to be so. Unlike his contemporary, the author Thomas Hamilton, who thought the country "too new for a landscape painter," Porter urged his readers to look about and "imitate the natural appearance" of the things they saw.

His credo appeared in an 1845 issue of *Scientific American*: "There can be no scenery found in the world which presents a more gay and lively appearance in a painting, than an American farm, on a swell of land, and with various colored fields well arranged." Earlier, in 1841, he had written in the *New York Mechanic* that earth had no fairer sight than an American farm "presenting the appearance of thrift and life." Almost as pleasing to Porter was

# Nineteenth-Century Villas

the sight of a factory built beside a rapid or waterfall, with "one or two mechanical shops, showing the water wheels, by which the machinery may be supposed to move." Wild, romantic scenery, then fashionable in conventional American landscape painting, had no place in Porter's heart or, presumably, in the hearts of ordinary Americans. In their parlors and bedrooms they wanted only manifestations of, as Porter's biographer Jean Lipman put it, peace, prosperity, and industry.

Itinerant painters, possibly from New England, also plied their trade in Nova Scotia, New England's Maritime neighbor. In the parlor of a simple Cape Cod cottage in the village of Granville Ferry, near Annapolis Royal, were found two wall-high paintings, executed in 1846: One is a view of London, the other of St. Petersburg. Other, smaller paintings show a ship launching in Nova Scotia, a hunter and his dog, a landscape with waterfall, and a Micmac Indian family.

Both city scenes, which were painted in deep perspective, present the weighty civic and religious architecture of European capitals. The London view shows the National Gallery, the church of St. Martin in the Fields, and the walk around Trafalgar Square; the St. Petersburg view shows the River Neva and St. Isaac's Cathedral. Both are simplified versions of wood engravings in early issues of the immediately popular *Illustrated London News*, launched in May of 1842. To link the two views, and so form a near-continuous city landscape, the skylines were aligned, and, to match the watery expanse of the River Neva, prominent in the painting of St. Petersburg, Trafalgar Square was filled with water.

Wood engravings from the *Illustrated London News* were also models for two of the remaining paintings: the landscape with waterfall, and the hunter and his dog—actually His Royal Highness Prince Albert "buck shooting" in the Scottish highlands. The painter, as was usually the case, left no signature. According to the lore of the Croscup family, he was a runaway sailor, but in Nova Scotia, as in New England, most wall paintings where the painter was unknown were attributed to wandering sailors, prisoners of the 1812 war, or the local drunk.

Despite the enormous popularity of pictures, wall paintings and panoramic papers fell out of favor during the second half of the nineteenth century. Dufour and Zuber had few imitators, and by 1867 the two had produced the last of their great scenics. Machine, or cylinder, printing, favored repeating designs that were easily matched. Simple abstract or geometrical designs quickly ousted pictures. By the last quarter of the century cheap, machine-printed "run of the mill" papers were the universal wallcovering. Abstract patterning was also encouraged by design critics who taught an

Itinerant wall painters were also active in British North America. One wall of the parlor of the Croscup house in Granville Ferry, Nova Scotia, showed a ship launching in a bustling harbor. The horse race along the shore is less incongruous than it seems. "Shore racing" was popular at the time, 1846. (National Gallery of Canada, Ottawa)

ever-widening audience to differentiate realistic from abstract patterns and to prefer the latter. Scenic papers, they charged, counted for too much in a room; they attracted interest when they should only have been background, and they belied the flatness and solidity of the wall. A critic at the New York Crystal Palace Exhibition (1853) pronounced that elaborate papers might be admissible in public halls and saloons, and even in the entranceways of private residences, but private drawing rooms, libraries, or chambers were strictly out of bounds. "Landscapes . . . whether large or small, groups or figures . . . should be carefully avoided in paper hangings . . . . Few things are more unpleasing to a cultivated eye than the bunches of gaudy flowers and foliage perspectively rendered in the intensest colors, and landscapes, repeated with endless iteration on the walls."

The American public heeded the critics. By 1880 scenic wallpapers were so out of favor that only the foolhardy would hang them. The French, wrote

## Nineteenth-Century Villas

an admiring Clarence Cook in 1880, might permit themselves "full liberty" in the matter of decoration, imitating anything and everything they can; but he continued wistfully:

[Americans,] being I suppose at the very root more akin to the English than to the French, have blindly accepted the English dictum in this matter, and look upon wall-papers with any but set conventional patterns and sombre colors, as vulgar. . . . 'Tis as much as a man's reputation for good taste is worth, to confess that he likes to see a pretty flowered paper on a bed-room wall; and one can hardly estimate the courage it would take to own that one liked an old-fashioned landscape paper in a hallway or in a dining-room.

# Gardens Indoors

he desire to open up the walls of the house and admit the garden, either literally or figuratively, is a constant in the history of house design and decoration. Roman wall paintings, the Cyzicene, and the Elizabethan long gallery all spoke of a desire to merge living space with the garden. The outdoor triclinium, the tree house, and the summer house, which took the room outdoors, were expressions of the same desire. But to reverse the coin, to bring the garden physically indoors, proved more difficult. Until the Industrial Revolution, neither heating systems nor glazing and construction techniques were able to dispel interior cold and darkness. Hybrid areas where house and garden could meet and mingle were the gift of glass walls and roofs and steam and hot-water heating systems. Together, they fulfilled the age-old longing for a year-round or winter garden.

## GREENHOUSES AND

## CONSERVATORIES

The ancestors of the winter garden were heated buildings with solid roofs and large windows which were used to nurse citrus fruits and other "tender greens" through the northern winter. "Greenhouses" or "conservatories" were also used to accelerate, or "force," the growth of native plants. In 1629 John Parkinson recommended placing orange trees, the most fragrant and prized of the exotics, "in a house or close gallery in the winter time." As more and more exotics arrived, each with its own requirements for light and heat, separate greenhouses were built. Thus, by the beginning of the nineteenth century, a catholic collector and grower might have had an orangery, a vinery, a peach house, and a pinery (for pineapples) in addition to a greenhouse for general plants. The first all-glass structures were built after the middle of the eighteenth century.

From the outset some greenhouses were used for the display as well as the nurture of plants. If next to the house, the orangery, for example, served as a diversion for guests at banquets and summer fêtes. Trees—which at first were grown in tubs—were brought onto the lawns and grouped at will; within the orangery there were walkways and promenades for viewing the less moveable plants as well as seats for resting, reading, or taking light refreshment. For seventeenth-century horticulturist T. Langford, such greenhouses were descendants of summer houses and banqueting houses: "Greenhouses are of late built as ornaments to gardens as well as for a conservatory for tender plants, and when the curiosities in the summer time are dispersed in their proper places in the garden the [green]house . . . may serve for an entertaining room" (1696). Queen Anne used the orangery at Kensington Palace as a "summer supper house." Gradually, the words *greenhouse* and *conservatory* acquired different meanings: A greenhouse was a place for the propagation and growth of plants, a conservatory for their display.

Because of the high costs of glazing and construction, only the owners or controllers of large private or public purses could afford conservatories. The scale of the buildings tended to match the size of the purses; the very largest were nothing less than enclosed gardens. In 1802 Prince Potemkin attached to the end of his living quarters, in the palace of Taurida near St. Petersburg, a large semicircular building with tall vertical windows and a solid roof supported by pillars disguised as palm trees. The walks of the garden, noted Chevalier Storch, meandered "amidst flowering hedges and fruit bearing shrubs, winding over little hills and producing, at every step, fresh occasions for surprise."

**PUBLIC**

**WINTER GARDENS**

The first half of the nineteenth century also saw the building of public conservatories or "winter gardens" in most European capitals and large cities. The first opened in Berlin in the winter of 1813–14. From Europe, the idea of the winter garden spread to North America. San Francisco's palm house, in Golden Gate Park, was built in the 1870s from prefabricated wooden parts shipped around Cape Horn from England. New York City's Botanical Garden, "an American Kew," dates from 1891. The delight in winter gardens was palpable: "From the keen, frosty air outside, and the flowerless aspect of universal nature," exulted J. C. Loudon on the opening of the Regent's Park winter garden, "one steps into an atmosphere balmy and delicious and not in the slightest degree oppressive. The most exquisite odors are wafted to and fro with every movement of the glass doors. Birds singing in the branches . . . make you again and again pause to ask, is this winter? Is this England?"

In less rapturous mood, Loudon also pointed out that part of the pleasure of public winter gardens lay in their informal, "outdoor" arrangement. They had winding walks, fountains, plots of grass, and ponds. But though labeled, and carefully tended by legions of gardeners, the plants for the most part were merely decorative background. The gardens were chiefly meeting places where people walked, sat, or listened to music among the flowers, shrubs, and trees. Seats and moveable tables were scattered among the plants, and in the larger and more elaborate buildings there were separate saloons for billiards, cards, and private parties.

On winter mornings the gardens were male domains; in them men read newspapers, drank chocolate, talked politics, and—where permitted—smoked. By midafternoon the company was mixed: Both sexes strolled among the trees and shrubs or sat at tables, talking or reading and drinking punch, beer, coffee, or wine. Evenings were for theatergoers, who visited the gardens, which were illuminated, before going home. Besides living quarters for its gardeners, the Jardin d'Hiver in Paris had a ballroom, a cafe, and a reading room.

So fixed was the perception of large greenhouses and winter gardens as public or semipublic places that botanical winter gardens, built expressly to house tropical and subtropical plants, usually had to serve two purposes. Most felt obliged to admit visitors, and, in effect, they became public winter gardens. Kew, which at first had been closed to the public, opened its doors in 1841 with the completion of the palm house. The winter garden of the Royal Botanic Society, which opened in Regent's Park in London in 1846, admitted the public from the outset. Though the society's interests were scientific, and while space had been set aside for a lecture hall, library, and museum, the garden was as much a meeting place as a plant house. At the Toronto Horticultural Society's botanical garden, science yielded even more ground to society; a pavilion added in 1879 became the city's most fashionable ballroom and high-tea spot.

As if to acknowledge the social function of botanical gardens, plant arrangements within them were scenic rather than scientific. In early greenhouses plants were laid out systematically in botanical categories, but in the semipublic winter gardens, system yielded to scenery. Trees and shrubs were planted in irregular and often picturesque groups, not in ways that facilitated identification and classification. Inadvertently, Kew had given the lead by grouping plants as though they were in their natural habitats. But whereas at Kew and other botanical gardens the arrangements served the needs of plants and ecological accuracy, in the public winter gardens and the larger private ones they served the eye.

**DOMESTIC**

**CONSERVATORIES**

The conservatory, in its modern sense of a room for plants attached to a dwelling, dates from about 1760. To house his small collection of citrus trees, William Belchier, an Englishman, built a covering entirely of glass which could be entered from the house. A pair of folding glass doors led from his drawing room into a world where the trees were protected from the elements. In Cowper's words:

> Unconscious of a less propitious clime,
> There blooms exotic beauty warm and snug,
> While the winds whistle, and the rains descend.

By the nineteenth century, a practice that had begun as a mildly eccentric experiment had become a "mania." "From the beginning of the present century," wrote the anonymous compiler of *Famous Parks and Gardens* (1880), "a mania for conservatories has spread contagiously among all the richer classes of the cold or temperate countries of Europe. . . . In the towns and villages of Britain, they are attached to all the more pretentious houses— their bowers of foliage and blossom frequently communicating with the drawing or sitting room." Conservatories were also popular in the United States, even though the hotter, sunnier summers and generally colder winters made them more difficult to manage. But despite the need for canvas blinds and pulleys as protection against strong sunlight, by 1850 the manufacturers of greenhouses and conservatories in the Northeast had long lists of well-to-do customers.

Though the idea of a year-round garden appealed to everyone, conser-

Le Jardin d'Hiver, Lyon. By massing the plants in picturesque groups, the designers of the winter garden left ample space for walking and talking. (Musée Historique de Lyon)

vatories could never have become popular without improvements in glass technology and, in England, the removal of the glass tax in 1845. After midcentury, prices of basic sheet glass tumbled, bringing conservatories within the range of middle-class purses. Better rolling techniques increased the size of glass sheets, reducing both their cost and the number of ribs or glazing bars needed to hold them. The quality of glass also improved. Older glass had often been more translucent than transparent, and even when clear it was frequently bubbled. The bubbles, gardeners maintained, acted as burning glasses, singeing the plants.

At the same time, there were marked improvements in methods of construction and heating. Steam or hot water passed through cast-iron pipes gave a more even distribution of heat than open fires or wood and coal stoves. Winter rooms, for the first time in history, could now be flooded with natural light and kept warm. In Europe, the introduction of a malleable wrought-iron glazing bar, which could withstand bending and stress as well as pressure, also made possible a far greater variety of conservatory plans than when the glass had been held in rigid frames of cast iron or wood. Wood frames persisted only in the United States, where the greater expansion and contraction of the metal bars caused by colder winters and hotter summers tended to break the glass. The weakened joints also let in rain and cold air.

At first the manufacturers of conservatories produced complete buildings, but once iron makers discovered that building parts could be standardized and put together in any number of combinations, the designed conservatory gave way to the modular one. By the 1880s, parts could be ordered by mail and used with a variety of ground plans. Architects became superfluous.

A winter garden may have been an age-old dream, but in northern Europe at the end of the eighteenth century it had also become a practical necessity. Tender exotics arriving in unprecedented numbers from the tropics and subtropics had to be protected, and their owners naturally wished to display them in flattering and attractive surroundings. The solution was a heated conservatory in which the plants could either be housed in tubs or formal beds or arranged in irregular masses as in the natural landscape. Paths and drainage channels could be serpentine rather than straight, as could the lines of the wrought-iron glazing bars. To give the Botanic Gardens in Paris an even more natural look, the director suggested, in 1852, that the geometrical grid of windows might, through imaginative framing, be replaced by a more or less faithful imitation of the natural forms of branches.

Conservatory building also got a boost from fundamental changes in the design of houses. At the beginning of the nineteenth century, irregular, picturesque forms began to replace classical ones. In part, the changes were a result of changes in living arrangements. During the eighteenth century the main rooms of houses moved closer and closer to the ground, pushing servants' quarters—which had been at ground level—underground or out to the wings. As the main rooms descended, they acquired large (French) windows, reaching from ceiling to floor, which opened directly onto gardens and green lawns. The ideal arrangement, according to J. C. Loudon, was a garden laid out on the south or southeastern side of the house and linked to the rooms by verandas, pergolas, and trellises entwined with flowers and climbing creepers. French windows looked onto the garden, and when open, the scents and sounds of the garden would pass into the principal living rooms.

There were similar developments in the United States. In *The Art of Beautifying the Home Grounds* (1870), Frank J. Scott recommended that the house be made to appear to grow out of the landscape by planting shrubs

*Top,* Knowle Cottage, Sidmouth, Devon, built in 1805 and converted by its owner, Thomas L. Fish, into a "Truly Elegant Marine Villa Ornée." The informality of the design, its sensitivity to the contour, and the thatched roof combine to marry the building to its surroundings. *Bottom,* The drawing room at Knowle Cottage, 1834. The opened French windows, which reached to the ground, brought indoors the sounds and scents of the garden. (Both photos from Yale University Press)

and bushes around the foundation and vines and creepers along the walls. Shrubs, bushes, and lawns were to replace labor-intensive ornamental flower beds. To heighten the sense of unity, he also advised that the house be painted a color compatible with the surroundings, not the habitual white. Porches and covered dining areas, built onto sides of the house which faced gardens and the sun, were additional links between house and garden. After the Civil War sleeping porches proliferated, first in vacation houses and by the end of the century in suburban houses. Blinds or awnings kept out the rising sun and wire screens insects and flies. Encircled by sleeping porches, covered dining areas, and conservatories, the mid-nineteenth-century American house was a shell of transitional spaces surrounding a permanent indoor core.

In addition to the tacking on of irregular rooms or wings, there were internal departures from balanced, classical design. Asymmetry began with *cottages ornés* in the eighteenth century, and from these it spread to more conventional housing. The object of the departures was to suggest a building that had grown naturally or organically as distinct from one that had been created at a single stroke. Houses with irregular outlines and asymmetrical room plans could be fitted more easily into irregular landscapes. With no commitment to symmetry of facade, level skylines, or a balanced arrangement of rooms, picturesque neo-Gothic houses could be made to look as broken and irregular as circumstances required. Rooms could be of different sizes and shapes, they could be grouped irregularly to enjoy the sun or a view, and they could open into conservatories or onto lawns and gardens.

When the openings between rooms were unobstructed, as they often were in American houses, and when there were no boundary walls, fences, or hedges to obstruct the view, it was possible to feel oneself, as the architect Eugene C. Gardner put it in 1874, in the midst of "an all-surrounding beauty." In Gardner's houses the divisions between rooms and between inside and outside were deliberately blurred. Windows in the walls of angular-shaped rooms that projected into the garden brought the garden indoors almost as effectively as conservatories and banks of potted plants. The windows were large, and as well as facing gardens and the sun—during the hours when the room was most used—they were so placed that they afforded views from various points in the house, not just from a single room. By opening sliding doors, removing screens, and pushing back curtains, rooms could be thrown together to create one interconnected space.

It was this characteristic of American houses which disturbed Henry James when he visited his homeland in 1905. He remarked,

[There is a] diffused vagueness of separation between apartments, between hall and room, between one room and another, between the one you are in and the one you are not in, between the place of passage and the place of privacy. . . . Thus we see systematized the indefinite extension of all spaces and the definite merging of all functions; the enlargement of every opening, the exaggeration of every passage, the substitution of gaping arches and far perspectives and resounding voids for enclosing walls, for practicable doors, for controllable windows.

Early English exponents of irregular design and a more open layout were the architect John Nash and the landscape architect Humphry Repton. At the beginning of the nineteenth century they built two houses, at Luscombe and Sandridge in Devon, which took maximum advantage of the potentialities of the irregular house. In each of the houses the main rooms had windows down to the ground which were placed so as to frame the view in different directions. From the drawing room at Luscombe one could look either west across the park or south through a little conservatory and along a valley. At Sandridge the drawing room and the dining room were of different shapes, and each had French windows angled on views up and down the estuary of the Dart. The Sandridge house also had two conservatories, a small one opening into both the drawing room and the dining room and a large one opening from the hall and used to mask the servants' wing. To create the illusion of a "flower tunnel" running through the house, Repton advised conservatory owners to place a large mirror at the end of the house opposite the conservatory: "An enfilade, or visto, though a modern house, is occasionally increased by a conservatory at one end, and repeated by a large mirror at the opposite end."

Usually, the size of a conservatory was determined by the scale of the house. Most conservatories were small, but those in palatial houses could be a match for the public winter gardens. When King Ludwig II of Bavaria enlarged his living quarters in 1867, he added a glass-covered roof garden 600 feet long by 100 wide. The king was an avid collector of exotic plants and a financial backer of scientific botanical expeditions. The garden contained a pond, which was large enough for Ludwig to row on, a brook, a fountain, trees, a reed hut, and an Oriental pavilion made of bamboo and silk. To complete the illusion of a tropical paradise, he imported finely colored birds and, in the background, had painted a panorama of the Himalayas. There is no evidence that the king gilded the lily by employing—as J. C. Loudon had suggested for such gardens—"men of various exotic races, if possible from the countries of origin of the plants exhibited." To avert charges of frivolity,

Loudon added that as well as tending the gardens, the men should be used for "educational purposes."

Loudon's idea was not new. In eighteenth-century *fêtes champêtres*, designed to suggest remote regions of the world or bygone ages, servants and guests had been dressed in costume appropriate to the place and period. One of Carmontelle's illustrations for the design of the gardens at the Parc de Monceau in France shows servants dressed in central Asiatic costume leading a dromedary through a park. In the background is a Tartar tent. Exotic settings, whether indoors or out, lifted the spirits of Europamudes.

Some notion of the impact of winter gardens on European sensibilities may be gauged from Guy de Maupassant's description of one in *Bel Ami* (1885):

> They came at last to the drawing room, and the conservatory opened out before them, a large wintergarden full of tall trees from tropical countries sheltering massed groups of rare flowers. Stepping under that dark vegetation, where the light slipped through the leaves like a silver shower, one breathed the tepid freshness of the damp earth and a heavy perfume wafting across. It was a strange, sweet, sickly and delightful sensation of artificial nature, enervating and indolent. One walked across carpets like moss between solid masses of shrubs.

Though popular, indoor gardens did not please everyone. Humphry Repton may have liked the idea of a flower tunnel running through the house, but he preferred the illusion to the reality; he disliked the "damp smell of earth" and suggested that a lobby separate living quarters from conservatory. William Morris, with his dislike of "florist" plants, found conservatories alien and ugly and the growth in them quick and rank. They were also anathema to adherents of the new science of climatotherapy. General health, climatotherapists believed, was largely a function of the condition of the air. Healthy air was thought to be cool and dry, unhealthy air warm and wet. Least healthy of all was hot, humid air corrupted by poisons or "miasmata" exhaled by lush, decaying vegetation and bodies of standing water. Conservatories with ponds they regarded as veritable deathtraps. Loudon thought conservatories "useful in a medical point of view," but other writers would have none of them. Robert Kerr, author of *The Gentleman's House* (1864) and a firm defender of the climatotherapist faith, gave dire warning of the dangers that stalked a living room located next to a conservatory: "To be too directly attached to a Dwelling Room is inadvisable . . . the warm moist air, impregnated with vegetable matter and deteriorated by the organic action of plants, is both unfit to breathe and destructive of the fabrics of furniture and decoration."

# Gardens Indoors

To protect lungs and fabric from the rotting effects of damp air, and noses from the smell of earth, J. J. Stevenson, in *House and Architecture* (1880), urged that saloons, vestibules, galleries, and corridors be used as buffers between conservatories and drawing rooms, boudoirs and morning rooms. He bravely allowed that one of the drawing room windows might look directly into a conservatory. Alternatively, householders wanting to view the conservatory from a safe vantage point could, like the owner of Abbey Manor in Evesham, build a false mirror in the wall of the dining room. So seriously were the supposed dangers heeded that many conservatories had no access from the house at all; entry was from the garden only.

To the prurient, conservatories may also have been suspect on moral grounds. In his novel *La curée* (1872), Zola used the unrestrained growth of tropical plants, and their heavy, intoxicating scents, as metaphors for the uninhibited sexuality of the principals. The key scenes take place in the conservatory of a villa. Northern morals, as Byron's couplet reminds us, have always been suspect in tropical heat: "What men call gallantry and gods adultery / Is much more common where the climate's sultry."

Despite the proscriptions of moralists and climatotherapists, from the 1860s a conservatory or, at the very least, a glass porch was an indispensable adjunct to even a modest English or French villa. As most town and suburban gardens had no room for a separate building, the conservatory was usually attached to the house, but the desire to enlarge the living space and bring greenery indoors would in any case have taken precedence over any interest in horticulture or the well-being of the plants. True gardeners, of course, preferred a detached greenhouse, glassed on all sides, properly ventilated, and exposed to maximum sunlight. Woodward's, the American greenhouse and conservatory manufacturers, recommended that conservatories, which were designed chiefly for the display of plants when in bloom, need be exposed to sunlight for only about half the day.

Because they were assembled from prefabricated parts, conservatories could be added to existing houses or built into or onto new ones at no great cost and without great difficulty. Most were on ground floors or terraces; roof conservatories were comparatively rare. Modest ground-floor conservatories could not, of course, match the exotic splendor of King Ludwig's roof garden, but because iron could be cast or molded into almost any shape, householders could order designs for Chinese, Japanese, or Moorish gardens. If they also wanted birds, aviaries were easily attached.

To unite living space with both indoor and outdoor gardens, floors were sometimes covered with the same material as the floor of the conservatory, and the rooms themselves decorated with plants in pots, jardinieres, window boxes, and glass (Wardian) cases. Wicker furniture, made from osier or

Conservatory or winter garden built onto Shrubland Hall, Suffolk, in 1830. By 1860 most substantial houses had conservatories. (Courtesy, Royal Commission on the Historical Monuments of England)

# Gardens Indoors

willow wands left in their natural color or painted in soft shades of green and brown, echoed the varying shades of the living tree. In both Europe and the United States houses—in Virginia Woolf's phrase—became stifled with greenery. Potted plants invaded halls and stairways and, supported by trellises, trailed over walls and ceilings. In Europe great screens of flowers— *Zimmerlaube*, or room foliage—could cover entire walls. In the United States, "curtains" of flowers around windows that sometimes had a fringe of colored panes to recall the foliage outside were popular. In their book on the American home, Catherine Beecher and her sister Harriet Beecher Stowe described how slips of ivy immersed in bottles, flax seeds placed in wet sponges, and sweet potatoes laid in bowls of water would in due time make beautiful "verdant ornaments" capable of framing a window or making a green cornice along a ceiling.

Flowers, too, were often shown in association with an aquarium. When attending a party in Paris one hot summer evening in 1835, Fanny Trollope noted how "deliciously cool and agreeable" the rooms were. "The first was surrounded and decorated in all possible ways with a profusion of the most beautiful flowers, intermixed with so many large glass vases for gold fish, that I am sure the air was much cooled by evaporation from the water they contained."

**WARDIAN CASES**   The most ingenious interior decorations, however, were sealed glass cases—in effect miniature greenhouses—designed by Dr. Nathaniel Bagshaw Ward to protect delicate plants from the soot, dust, and noxious gases that laced the urban air. Even indoors the air could be so impure, especially after the introduction of gas lighting in the 1880s, that it was said that the only plant able to flourish without protection was the virtually indestructible aspidistra. According to his son Stephen, Dr. Ward was a keen and persevering naturalist, determined to realize *rus in urbe*, who had tired of trying to raise delicate plants in the smoke-charged air of London's East End. His antidote was a closely glazed case that kept pollutants out and moisture in.

In actuality, however, the discovery of the effectiveness of the sealed case appears to have been accidental. In 1829, wanting a perfect specimen of a hawk moth, Dr. Ward placed a chrysalis in some soil in a glass bottle and covered the opening with a lid. After a time, minute vegetation appeared on the surface of the soil which, with no assistance from Dr. Ward, eventually turned out to be a fern and a grass. The air, moisture, and nutrients required by the plants were contained within the bottle.

It soon became evident that the sealed glass cases, which eventually re-

The bay window of the sitting room in Colonel Custer's quarters at Fort Abraham Lincoln, ca. 1875. The Custers subscribed to the Victorian practice of converting the house into a veritable greenhouse of growing plants and vines. (Courtesy of Little Bighorn Battlefield National Monument)

placed the bottle, were tailor-made for transporting plants. On long ocean voyages unprotected plants were usually decimated by a combination of salt spray, dehydration, and fluctuations in temperature. But by shielding the plants from damaging elements and maintaining a consistent microclimate, the cases virtually guaranteed safe shipment. Ferns and grasses were shipped

# Gardens Indoors

A window curtained with plants, from *The American Woman's Home* by Catherine Beecher and Harriet Beecher Stowe, 1869. Between the ivy-filled floor planters is a Ward's case.

from Australia to England, tea plants from Shanghai to India, and bananas from China to Fiji and Samoa.

But it was as a parlor and drawing room decoration, not as a portmanteau for carrying plants, that most Victorians knew the Wardian case. Thanks to it, Stephen Ward proclaimed in a lecture at the Royal Institution, townspeople everywhere and at all times of the year could offset urban noise

**An elaborate Wardian case of the "Crystal Palace" type. Most cases were smaller than this, usually domes or bell jars that stood on fairly elaborate stands.**

and smells with living reminders of the freshness and beauty of the country. In addition, by filling their window wells with Wardian cases they could replace views of streets, backyards, canals, and tenements with "prospects of ferns and flowers." Though they could be bought for modest sums in a variety of shapes and sizes, Catherine Beecher and Harriet Beecher Stowe advised needy or thrifty Americans to make their own. As a further economy

**A tightly glazed glass dome, as illustrated in Nathaniel Ward's book** *On the Imitation of the Natural Conditions of Plants in Closely Glazed Cases* **(London, 1842).**

they urged the use of wild rather than greenhouse plants. A native fern, snug in its case, was "a fragment of the green woods brought in and silently growing."

In addition to Wardian cases, fashionable living rooms and drawing rooms might also have been decorated with artificial trees and shrubs. Trunk and stems were made of wood, foliage of leather. Through the stems ran narrow pipes that channeled gas to translucent glass fruits. When the gas was lighted, the effect, as one observer noted, was singularly charming: "a tree branching naturally, richly clothed in foliage, and hung with clusters of transparent, illuminated fruit." It reminded the observer of a scene of enchantment from the Arabian Nights. She could also have added a Persian court.

Though small prefabricated conservatories continued to be added to middle-class houses, by 1900 the heyday of conservatory building was over. Followers of the Arts and Crafts movement, which was rooted in the teachings of Ruskin and William Morris, disapproved of so artificial a barrier be-

The Toronto Winter Garden Theatre, meticulously restored by the Ontario Heritage Foundation and reopened in 1989. Pillars disguised as massive tree trunks support the proscenium, balconies, and roof; to complete the illusion of a forest glade, thousands of preserved, painted, and fireproofed beech leaves hang from the ceiling. (Photo courtesy of The Ontario Heritage Foundation; Hill Peppard, photographer)

tween house and garden. People, too, were moving outdoors at such a pace that Zephine Humphrey, in a delightful *Atlantic Monthly* essay (1916), feared for the passing of indoors. With "shivering regret" she watched soup cool and gravy congeal in outdoor dining rooms and felt her nose going numb in chilly, year-round sleeping porches, and she sighed for "indoors, dear indoors!" But with health, beauty, and longevity as the prizes, hardier spirits were not to be put off. Fresh air, declared the editors of the *Craftsman* (1914), an American magazine committed to the movement outdoors, was a better elixir than anything physicians could brew and seal in a bottle. In what amounted to a triumph for climatotherapy, a suntan, not the lily-white pallor admired by Victorians and Edwardians, became the most desired skin color. The liking for the feel of wind and sun on the skin gave the open-sided loggia an advantage over the closed, and sometimes stifling, conservatory. A skillfully designed loggia using vine-covered trellises could, while being out of doors, still provide a sense of enclosure. And in a world of rising labor and fuel costs, loggias required little upkeep and needed no heating. A great many conservatories, therefore, were either dismantled, converted into loggias, or allowed to decay.

The great public winter gardens also fell into disuse, for many of the same reasons. But in colder parts of the world, the idea of the winter garden, of a demi-paradise, survived until the eve of the Great War. In 1914 a winter garden theater opened in Toronto. The walls of the auditorium, and of the crush space behind, were painted with garden scenes in gay summer profusion. Huge artificial trees, with trunks of rough plaster, supported the balcony and the proscenium. The branches trailed off into painted ceilings covered with masses of hanging leaves and blossoms illuminated by both lanterns and concealed lights. The foliage, part real and part fake, was intended to rustle in breezes created by air, pouring through large side windows and roof ventilators, which was stirred by electric fans. But a fairyland that might have enchanted Victorian and Edwardian audiences was out of step with the tempered, post–World War I imagination. Vaudeville, too, had lost its appeal, and by 1921 the darkened theater was showing only films.

# Epilogue

he decline of the conservatory and the winter garden signaled a retreat from nature in interior decoration which has continued to the present. Most of us now live within plain, monochromatic walls, sit in plain, unpatterned chairs and sofas, and walk upon carpets that only occasionally remind us of exotic gardens. A French designer who, out of whimsy, dared to use garden motifs in a room at a New York City exhibition in the late 1930s was set upon by American colleagues for creating, as one of his assailants put it, "a riot of birds and bees and flowers that would be the despair of anyone but a botanist."

As motifs in decoration, gardens and landscapes suffered from our preoccupation with technology. This was already strong by the middle of the nineteenth century. The great public winter gardens, "cathedrals of glass" or "crystal palaces," were as much objects of wonder as the plants they housed; *the* Crystal Palace, built for the Great Exhibition of 1851, was a showplace that outshone its contents. Few Victorians had misgivings about technology despite the woeful condition of the industrial towns and cities. Living standards were higher in the city than in the country, pollution was still local, and, though cities were growing apace, there were as yet no megalopolises or conurbations. Technology, with its glittering manufactures and promise of release from grinding labor, was generally thought an unqualified good.

Tendencies within the arts and sciences also militated against naturalism. The microscope and the telescope undermined confidence in the naked eye by demonstrating that the appearance of things often masked essential form. Art that merely copied appearances no longer satisfied. What mattered, in art as in science, was "significant," not natural, form. In science the future lay with the diagram and the formula; in art, with abstraction.

There were related revolutions in architecture and interior decoration. A machine-based culture in search of significant form had little tolerance for decoration or ornament. Technology meant precise function, a weeding out of inessentials. When it became evident that machine production could not be halted, and that William Morris workshops were not tokens of the future, the attack on decoration was relentless. It began with architecture. The Chicago architect Louis Sullivan remarked in the 1890s that the rejection of ornament would allow architects to "concentrate entirely on the erection of buildings . . . finely shaped and charming in their sobriety." The new building materials—steel girders and reinforced concrete—did not, in any case, encourage frills. Plain linear or angular forms were the hallmarks of new construction. Beauty became identified with the useful or the functional: the clean lines of a skyscraper, the carefully calculated curves of a transatlantic liner, the streamlines of an automobile.

The most outspoken enemy of decoration was Adolf Loos, the Czechborn but Vienna-based architect. In a 1908 essay, "Ornament and Crime," he denounced ornament as a form of primitivism and equated cultural advance with its removal from utilitarian objects. Ornament's "crime" was to waste society's resources, of both money and time, on the unnecessary and the archaic. Loos's objections were directed chiefly at exteriors; he himself built plain white cubelike buildings with traditional interiors. But other architects and designers, for whom Loos had provided a rationale, went further. Turning his argument inside out, they designed interiors that were just as austere as Loos's exteriors. Walls were undecorated, lighting unsoftened, and floors left bare.

Architects of a more traditional bent may have flinched at Loos's vehemence and questioned the austerities of some of his followers, but virtually all embraced the message. Out of it grew a rationalized, sharp-edged, machine-based style that crossed all national boundaries. The International Style, as Mies van der Rohe put it, had no decoration, "no noodles or armoured turrets." Unlike previous styles, it made no distinction between structure and decoration. Its province was the complete building and its objective, as members of the famous Bauhaus school of design put it, *Gesamtkunstwerk*—the total, integrated, consistent design. The style's most celebrated exponent, Le Corbusier, declared in 1923 that his goal was to reject decorative art and "affirm that architecture extends from the smallest furnishing to the house, to the street, to the city, and beyond." Rejecting an earlier tendency to translate natural forms into architectural ones, he subsumed design within the new materials and the new techniques. His objective was to show that by adopting the principles of machine production, an architect could produce forms that were as "neat, clear, [and] clean" as steamships and airplanes. In dwellings, his ideal was a standardized unit, a "house-tool" that would combine comfort and beauty with efficiency: "a practicable habitable cell . . . a veritable machine for habitation."

A machine/dwelling had no room for decoration, only "equipment," and this standardized. Fantasists even dispensed with chairs, replacing them with rising currents of air strong enough to support a reclining human. Though people resisted the excesses of the purists, interiors were simplified. Walls painted in a single color replaced papered ones, and furnishings became spare, functional, and impersonal. Ornament was rejected on hygienic as well as aesthetic grounds. William Morris delivered his first public attack on excessive ornament at a conference on public hygiene in 1884. Lightness and whiteness were seen as adjuncts to health; dust was deemed dangerous, and objects that harbored it were banished. The ideal habitat was a "dustless home." A healthy room was a clinically bare one. Embroidered wall hangings, heavy curtains, tablecloths, and potted plants—all the things that made Victorians feel at home—preyed on modern sensibilities.

As well as being out of place in the new interiors, plants and garden- or landscape-inspired decoration were no longer necessary. Travel, which had become easier, and photographs and film satisfied needs once filled by scenic wallpapers and wall paintings. There was also a greater tolerance for cities; conditions within them improved, and city-bred inhabitants began to outnumber migrants from rural areas. Nostalgia for the countryside abated, and the city, which recovered some of its preindustrial aura, for many became the preferred environment. But the most notable change was in the quality of interiors. For the first time in history these were warm and well lighted. Central heating, glass, and electric lighting had dispelled interior cold and darkness. Thomas Edison's incandescent light represented, as one admirer remarked, a "victory over night." There were also victories over daytime lighting, which had never been brilliant. When walls had carried the roof, window spaces tended to be tall and narrow, but walls that were mere coverings for frames of wood, steel, or reinforced concrete could be pierced at will. Whitened ceilings and large windows filled with sheets or plates of transparent glass brightened interiors. Furnishings may have suffered a little, but fading fabrics no longer mortify, and modern dyes are, in any case, much less fugitive in sunlight.

The logic of the new materials suggested a window at eye level running the whole width of the room. But buildings could, if desired, be walled entirely with glass. As a result, rooms that might once have been as dark as caves were flooded with light. They also became windows on the world. A view worth looking at became part of the interior decoration, so that actual landscapes seen through a glass wall or a large "picture window" tended to replace painted, sewn, or woven ones. A living room with a wall decorated by the best Artist of all, noted the editors of *Sunset* magazine, needed only a vase of wildflowers for decoration. In California, where—as elsewhere in the United States—houses had always been "set straight" on their rectangular lots, a few were built boldly on the bias to take advantage of a view.

Wall paintings and hangings with landscape subjects are now used consistently only in rooms without windows. They were standard features, for example, in underground houses built in the United States in the 1960s and 1970s. Though surrounded by an earth-covered concrete shell, the houses had conventional windows that served as conduits for their circulation systems. Some of the windows looked onto courtyard gardens, lit artificially, and some onto landscapes painted with luminous paints on the walls of the surrounding shell. Thanks to ingenious lighting systems, simulations of early dawn light, full sunlight, dusk, and moonlight could be summoned by the flick of a switch. From the living room window of a house in the Rocky Mountains, built underground on a mountaintop some 9,000 feet above sea level, the view was of the Hudson River backed by the Manhattan skyline.

"Dream world images," to quote Jay Swayze, a designer and builder of underground houses, were also painted on garden walls and other "outdoor" surfaces. At night these were lit by an artificial moon that shone from a star-studded velvet sky; by day gardens and paintings basked in the equivalent of full sunlight. To provide the sound, feel, and fragrance of an outdoor setting, the gardens were equipped with small pools and waterfalls, living trees, shrubs, and flowers. Nature itself, remarked Swayze, could not have done it so well.

Dream worlds were also available to people who lived above ground. By dissolving the barriers between indoors and outdoors, stationary or sliding walls of glass fulfilled the promise of the Cyzicene and the French window. The idea of space as a single flowing entity uninterrupted by structural walls was the gift of Frank Lloyd Wright. Capitalizing on tendencies long present

# Epilogue

A contemporary American living room. The floor-level deck and encircling trees, seen through a glass wall, are an extension of the room. Exposed roof rafters, prominent shelving, and piled hearth logs bring the world of wood literally indoors. (Ernest Braun, with permission)

in the design of American houses, he brought the landscape up to the walls of the house with urns and planters and took the house into the landscape by means of projecting walls and long interior vistas that seemed to flow outward through rows of windows into the surrounding space. Where this was unwooded prairie or open suburban landscape of lawns, foundation plantings, and low shrubs, interior and exterior space formed an unbroken continuum. Bricks, tiles, and stones, whose colors and textures echoed the soil, and which were exposed indoors as well as out, completed the marriage of house and landscape. Urns and planters, too, usually echoed some feature of the house, and by doing so they carried the spirit of the architect into the garden.

The integration of interior and exterior space is now a standard feature of modern design, particularly in warm and sunny parts of the world. In house design, the American Margaret Goldsmith wrote emphatically in 1941, there were two guiding ideas: "*to bring the out-of-doors into the living rooms*" and "*to carry the living rooms out of doors.*" Living rooms were routinely oriented to take advantage of sunlight and the most attractive outdoor spaces, even if it meant relegating them to the back of the house. Large windows and sliding glass doors brought the garden indoors, and porches, pergolas, and patios carried the living space into the garden. Turn-of-the-century California, America's "Mediterranean," led the way. In one of the first issues of *Sunset* magazine, a contributor (Ernest Peixotto), who had returned to California after a long sojourn in Italy, appealed for a vernacular architecture. Instead of Queen Anne cottages with cupolas, tiny windows, balustrades, and other gewgaws he called for "houses with fair open fronts and windows large enough to freely admit [California's] warm Italian sunlight. . . . Everything [in California] conduces to the enjoyment of an out-door life—in other words of a healthful life."

*Sunset*, published originally by the Southern Pacific Railway Company, by the end of the First World War was a truly national magazine taking, through its column "The Home in the West," California's message to the entire continent. In the Northeast the cry of the outdoors was taken up by the *Craftsman*, *Sunset*'s sister organ: "Real homes," *Craftsman*'s editors noted in 1914, "not just city houses, must have an outdoor room, a fragrant place under shady trees or a blue vault of sky, the 'walls' hung with living tapestries, vines and roses, with a green grass carpet,—a place in which one can really live, rest, sleep, breathe, dine and meet friends."

For societies taking to the outdoors the one-story bungalow, the near-universal suburban form, was an ideal instrument. An Indian or Bengali house type modified by the English, it had from the first provided relief from the city—bungalows were usually built in the hills—and the heat of the plains. Even when built in cities it was always considered a nonurban form and associated with a symbolic return to rural life. In both the new world and the old, it freed architects from European conventions, and because it obeyed no strict architectural rules, it could be adapted to local climates and cultures. In the United States a loose arrangement of rooms around a

A view of the deck and the sliding doors of the living room. The deck, which virtually surrounds the house, is also accessible from the dining room and bedrooms. (Ernest Braun, with permission)

An outdoor room, with a canopy of trees, in the Pacific Northwest. (Photograph by Don Normark)

# Epilogue

central living area satisfied an ideal of family life;* in warm climates a plan that allowed one room to be joined to the next facilitated through ventilation. As the progenitor of the original veranda, the bungalow, too, easily accommodated porches, pergolas, and sun rooms—those friendly "architectural hyphens," as the *Craftsman* put it, which link house and garden. With no steps or stairs to negotiate, its occupants could move freely between indoors and outdoors without being, thanks to the "hyphens," conscious of the transition. Like the Cape Cod house, an old colonial form, the bungalow hugged the ground. From southern California, its true occidental home, it spread quickly eastward and northward.

The perception of the garden as extra living space rather than as a setting for the house inevitably changed its form. Gardens had been treated as extensions of the house since Roman times, but always they were ornaments to be admired for their color, their patterns, and their scents. But in a world where doing is more important than looking, the garden has become ever more functional, its form determined less by the needs of the plants than by the organization of the house and the needs of its occupants. Trimming and mowing with batteries of power tools, not horticulture, are today's commonplace skills.

As outdoor rooms gardens required privacy, thus breaking, in the United States, the old taboo against fencing and hedging. Front gardens still form a continuous greensward, but the yards at the back are usually enclosed. Grass and native ground cover have extended their domains, and trouble-free perennials and shrubs, arranged naturalistically along the borders, have replaced beds of regimented annuals. Potted plants, which are easy to care for and arrange, have also become prominent. But in many gardens there may be very few flowers of any kind. More than ever before is the suburban property, in Frank J. Scott's phrase, "a haven of repose" in which relaxation and recreation are the order of the day. Very often, the suburban or town house garden is little more than a lawn, with a surround of perennials, or a quick-drying brick platform, studded with plants, on which lawn or garden furniture can be moved around at will. The ideal is a trim, easily maintained space that can be used for as long as the weather is warm and dry.

Though flowers, herbs, cottages, and picturesque countrysides no longer dominate walls and furnishings, it would take a brave observer to sound the death knell on gardens and landscapes as vital sources for motifs in decoration. Confidence in technology is no longer the immoveable faith it used to be; nor are people as enchanted with technology's hard, machined products.

---

*According to late nineteenth-century lore, in far-off colonial days the entire family is thought to have lived contentedly around the hearth of a single, large room, in which it prepared food, ate, and relaxed.

**A modern, "easy-care" garden in California. The features are standard: a lawn, a surround of perennials, shade trees, wooden decks, paved walkways, and a patio. (Darrow Watt, with permission)**

By the 1950s Le Corbusier himself had begun to relent, returning to the interest in texture, pattern, and the properties of materials which had marked his formative years. Austere interiors and walls of glass, two of the icons of modernism, have lost ground. Rooms walled with uncurtained sheets of glass can be seen into as well as out of; glass walls reduce privacy, and they may allow indoors unwanted aspects of the outdoors. All too often a picture window looks onto a nondescript street or a wintry yard, and after dark it merely registers a dark hole. By fixing attention on the window itself rather than on the outlook beyond, sash bars are at least a reminder, as William Morris remarked, that we are indoors and have a roof over our heads.

Disenchantment with technology and the current interest in ecology and environment have also heightened enthusiasm for both outdoor and indoor gardening. Plants have been making their way indoors on such a scale that

# Epilogue

there is now a profession—"interiorscaping" or "plantscaping"—to select, arrange, and accommodate them. Leafy, tropical plants are popular decorations for covered shopping malls, hotel foyers, restaurants, and offices. Atriumlike spaces have made successful restaurants and dining rooms, and trees planted in rows have given indoor shopping malls a streetlike effect. In offices, plants are used to soften the effects of hard materials and to create areas of privacy. Domestic conservatories, too, are flourishing. They are a good deal smaller than they used to be, but there are so many of them that, collectively, they probably house more plants than did conservatories in their nineteenth-century heyday. There are signs, too, that flowers and other plants are making a comeback in contemporary fabrics and wallpapers. Yet despite the renewed interest in naturalistic decoration, it seems unlikely that rooms will ever again be bowers of branches and strewn herbs and flowers or that walls will be covered with representations of trees, forests, and countrysides. But by the same token we clearly have no desire to live without some connection to the organic world or, as Cowper might have put it, without something of the country around us.

# Bibliography

Any study of nature and landscape as motifs in decoration and design rests upon two seminal works: Joan Evans' *Pattern* (Oxford University Press, 1931) and *Nature in Design* (Oxford University Press, 1933). They are books of remarkable range and depth, and though no longer young, they are still fresh and vibrant. Joan Evans' ideas on decoration reverberate throughout this book.

Because the study was neither strictly one of decoration nor of gardens and landscapes, but of the relationship between them, books that examined ways in which we have perceived the natural world were especially useful. Two were indispensable: Derek Pearsall and Elizabeth Salter's *Landscapes and Seasons of the Medieval World* (University of Toronto Press, 1973) and Keith Thomas's wonderfully encyclopaedic, but also analytical, *Man and the Natural World* (Pantheon, 1983). More limited in scope, but no less penetrating, were A. R. Humphreys' *Augustan World* (Methuen, 1954) and Pat Rogers' *Augustan Vision* (Weidenfeld, 1972).

Of the specialists works on interiors, the most useful were those that examined decoration and design in a context of social and cultural history. An early and fine example of the genre is Phyllis Ackerman's *Tapestry: A Mirror of Civilization* (Oxford University Press, 1933). Later examples among books on tapestry are André Lejard's *French Tapestry* (Elek, 1946), Pierre Verlet's *Book of Tapestry* (Edita S. A. Lausanne, 1965), F. P. Thompson's *Tapestry: Mirror of History* (David & Charles, 1980), Roger d'Hulst's *Flemish Tapestries from the Fifteenth to the Eighteenth Century* (Editions Arcade, 1967), and Roger Armand Weingert's *French Tapestry* (Faber, 1962). For the significance of the hunt in tapestries, *Connoisseur* offers two fine articles: Donald King's "Devonshire Hunts: Art and Sport in the Fifteenth Century" (196:80, 1977), and Derek Pearsall's "Hunting Scenes in Mediaeval Illuminated Manuscripts" (196:79, 1977). For readers specifically interested in the Devonshire tapestries, an instructive source is *The Devonshire Hunting Tapestries* by G. W. Digby and W. Helford (HMSO, 1971).

Writings on embroidery are a rich source of domestic and garden history. Thomasina Beck's delightful *Embroidered Gardens* (Viking, 1979) is, no pun intended, groundbreaking and definitive. In it she acknowledges the broadening influence of her mentor Joan Edwards, author of the thoughtful *Crewel Embroidery in England* (William Morrow, 1975). Rozsika Parker's *Subversive Stitch* (Women's Press, 1984) is a provocative and scholarly history of embroidery written from a feminist point of view. Older, traditional histories worth consulting are George Wingfield Digby's *Elizabethan Embroidery* (Faber, 1963), Margaret Jourdain's *History of English Secular Embroidery* (Kegan Paul, 1910), Therle Hughes' *English Domestic Needlework* (Macmillan, 1961), and Lanto Synge's *Antique Needlework* (Blandford, 1988).

One of the earliest books on wallpaper is Clarence Cook's *What Shall We Do with Our Walls* (Warren Fuller, 1880); it is still stimulating. Nancy McClelland's *Historic Wallpapers* (Lippincott, 1924) and Phyllis Ackerman's *Wallpaper: Its History, Design and Use* (Stoke, 1933) have also weathered extremely well. More recent studies are E. A. Entwhistle's *French Scenic Wallpapers* (F. Lewis, 1972), Catherine Lynn's *Wallpaper in America* (Norton, 1980), Brenda Greysmith's *Wallpaper* (Macmillan, 1976), and two comprehensive surveys: *Wallpapers: An International History and Illustrated Survey* by Charles C. Oman, Jean Hamilton, and Harry M. Abrams (Abrams, 1982) and *Wallpaper: A History* by Françoise Teynac, Pierre Nolot, and Jean-Denis Vivien (Thames & Hudson, 1982).

Wall painting in the United States is comprehensively covered by Nina Fletcher Little's *American Decorative Wall Painting, 1700–1850* (Dutton, 1972) and Jean Lipman's books on Rufus Porter, the prolific New England wall painter: *Rufus Porter, Yankee Pioneer* (Clarkson N. Potter, 1968) and *Rufus Porter Rediscovered* (Clarkson N. Potter, 1980). Wall painting in England is the subject of a two-volume study by Edward Croft-Murray: *Decorative Painting in England* (Country Life, 1962). The wall paintings found at Granville Ferry, Nova Scotia, are analyzed by Gilbert L. Gignac and Jeanne L'Esperance in their article "Thoughts of Peace and Joy: A Study of the Iconography of the Croscup Room" (*Journal of Canadian Art History* 6:2, 1982).

On the appeal and influence of the Orient, Hugh Honour's *Chinoiserie: The Vision of Cathay* (Harper & Row, 1961) is the most telling work. It is supplemented by Oliver Impey's *Chinoiserie: The Impact of Oriental Styles on Western Art and Decoration* (Oxford University Press, 1977). John Irwin unlocked the secrets of chintz in his *Burlington Magazine* article entitled "Origins of the Oriental Style in English Decorative Art" (97, 1955) and, with Katherine Brett, in *Origins of Chintz* (HMSO and the Victoria and Albert

# Bibliography

Museum, 1970). For the cultural significance of gardens in Persia and their influence on early carpet design, general readers need go no further than Arthur Upham Pope's *Introduction to Persian Art* (Peter Davies, 1930) and *Survey of Persian Art* (Oxford University Press, 1939).

The literature on gardens and flowers is very large. General studies useful to my purpose were Marie Luise Gothein's *History of Garden Art* (J. M. Dent, 1913), Nan Fairbrother's *Men and Gardens* (Knopf, 1956), Eleanour Sinclair Rhode's *Story of the Garden* (Hale, Cushman & Flint, 1926), Anthony Huxley's *Illustrated History of Gardening* (Paddington, 1978), Derek Clifford's *History of Garden Design* (Faber, 1962), Ronald King's *Quest for Paradise* (Whittet, 1979), Christopher Thacker's *History of Gardens* (Croom Helm, 1979), Peter Coates' *Flowers in Their History* (Viking, 1970), and J. B. Jackson's luminous essays on gardens in *The Necessity for Ruins* (University of Massachusetts Press, 1980).

Of garden studies restricted to particular times or places, the most valuable were Wilhelmina Jashemski's *Gardens of Pompeii* (Caratzas, 1979), Sir Frank Crisp's *Medieval Gardens* (Hacker, 1976), Eleanour Sinclair Rohde's *Shakespeare's Wildflowers* (Medici Society, 1935), Edmund Gosse's "Elizabethan Flower-Gardens" (*Harper's Monthly*, June 1905, pp. 139–146), Maurice Maeterlinck's *Old Fashioned Flowers* (Dodd, Mead, 1905), Alicia Amherst's *History of Gardening in England* (Bernard Quaritch, 1896), and Terry Comito's *Idea of the Garden in the Renaissance* (Rutgers University Press, 1978). Older American gardens are the subject of two fine books by Ann Leighton: *American Gardens of the Eighteenth Century* (University of Massachusetts Press, 1976) and *American Gardens of the Nineteenth Century* (University of Massachusetts Press, 1987). The new American garden is analyzed in a book of the same name by Caroline Ottesen (Macmillan, 1987).

On indoor gardens, the most comprehensive studies are Stefan Koppelkaum's *Glasshouses and Wintergardens of the Nineteenth Century* (Granada, 1981) and Georg Kohlmaier and Barna von Sartory's *Houses of Glass* (MIT Press, 1986). Shorter studies are Alexander Bartholomew's *Conservatories and Garden Rooms* (MacDonald, 1985) and Priscilla Boniface's *Garden Room* (HMSO, 1982). Readers specifically interested in Wardian cases may turn to Shirley Hibberd's *Rustic Adornments for Homes of Taste* (Groombridge, 1856).

Of books on domestic interiors in general, I am particularly indebted to David P. Handlin's *American Home* (Little, Brown, 1979) and Witold Rybzcinski's *Home: A Short History of an Idea* (Viking, 1986).

Authoritative modern studies of historic interiors are Margaret Wood's *English Mediaeval House* (Phoenix House, 1965); Peter Thornton's *Seventeenth-Century Interior Decoration in England, France and Holland* (Yale University Press, 1978); *Authentic Decor: the Domestic Interior, 1620–1920* (Viking, 1984); John Cornforth's *Quest for Comfort: English Interiors, 1790–1848* (Barrie & Jenkins, 1978); James Chambers' *English House* (Methuen, 1985); Mark Girouard's *Life in the English Country House* (Yale University Press, 1978); and Gail Caskey Winkler and Roger W. Moss's *Victorian Interior Decoration: American Interiors, 1830–1900* (Henry Holt, 1986). Older studies of interiors well worth reading are T. Hudson Turner's *Domestic Architecture in England* (Oxford University Press, 1851) and Nathaniel Lloyd's *History of the English House* (Architectural Press, 1931). On the influence of William Morris on interiors, the most valuable source was Roderick Marshall's *William Morris and His Earthly Earthly Paradises* (Compton Press, 1978).

On the spirit of modern interiors, and the modern movement in general, Robert Hughes' penetrating analysis of modern art, *The Shock of the New* (Knopf, 1981), was a stimulating source. Also useful were *The New Interior Decoration* by Dorothy Todd and Raymond Mortimer (Scribner's, 1929) and C. Ray Smith's comprehensive *Interior Design in Twentieth-Century America* (Harper & Row, 1987). The rise of the bungalow and its proliferation are well documented in Robert Winters' *California Bungalow* (Hennessey & Ingalls, 1980).

Two rich and informed sources of information on twentieth-century interiors and gardens are the popular American magazines *Craftsman* and *Sunset*. Publication of *Craftsman* ended in 1917, but *Sunset* flourishes still and remains a powerful influence on house and garden design in the United States. Indispensable, too, was yet another southwestern-based magazine: the inimitable *Landscape*, founded in 1951 by J. B. Jackson. For the meaning of gardens and landscapes in this and in other centuries, there could hardly be a more valuable or engaging source. And for anyone stepping gingerly across academic disciplines, which tend to be decidedly territorial, it is both a guide and an inspiration. *Landscape* essays that were especially valuable, either as catalysts or as sources of information, were Jurgis Baltrusaitis's "Land of Illusion—China and the Eighteenth Century Garden" (11:2, 1961), Robert Riley's "Emperor and the Virgin" (16:2, 1967), Geoffrey Grigson's "Room Outdoors" (4:2, 1954), J. B. Jackson's "Abstract World of the Hotrodder" (7:2, 1957), and Christopher Grampp's "Gardens for California Living" (28:3, 1985).

# Index

*Numbers in italics refer to illustrations.*

Ackerman, Phyllis, 89, 132
Adam of St. Victoire, 17
Addison, Joseph: and overseas commerce, 67; and improvements to estates, 95; and formal gardens, 95
Alberti, Leon Battista, 38
Albertus Magnus, 18
Alcinoüs, garden of, 2, 34, 96
Alexander the Great, 13
Alison, Rev. Archibald, 90
Animals, symoblism of, 55
Arras work. *See* Tapestries
Arts and Crafts Movement, 163
*Atlantic Monthly*, 165
Aubrey, John, 50
Austen, Jane, 95
Austen, Ralph, 46

Bacon, Francis: and gardens, 41; and knots, 42; and ornamental lake, 65
Balzac, Honore de, 134
Banks, Sir Joseph, 85
Banqueting houses, 45, 148
Barker, Robert, 116, 130
Barrell, John, 104
Bayeux tapestry, 29, 50
Beck, Thomasina: and gardening and embroidery, 61; and Berlin woolwork, 121; and William Morris, 125
Bedding out, 118–19; and knot gardens, 118, 119
Beecher, Catherine, 159, 162–63
*Bel Ami*, 156

Belchier, William, 150
Berenson, Bernard, 8
Berlin woolwork, 119–20; and carpet bedding, 121; and "leaf embroidery," 121
Berry, duc de, 76
Blackwork, and knot gardens, 62
Blair, Hugh, 97
Blondel, Jean Francois, 89
Boccacio, Giovanni, 21
Boler, James, 59, 82
Books of hours, as sources of decorative motifs, 25
"Boston Common" embroideries, 106, *107*
*Botanical Cabinet*, 111
*Botanical Magazine*, 111
Botany: and plant morphology, 56; and influence on embroidery, 56–59; as study for embroiderers, 109–11
Briconnet, Cardinal, 37
*Broderies par terre*, 65
Brontë, Charlotte, 123
Brown, Capability, 18
Budding, Thomas, 121
Buigne, Gace de la, 32
Bungalow: origins of, 172; versatility and dispersion of, 172–75
Byron, Lord, 157

California: and scenic wallpaper, 133; and picture windows, 170; and Mediterranean climate, 172; and *Sunset* magazine, 172; and the bungalow, 175; and gardens, *176*
Calverley, Lady Julia, and embroidered screens, 103–4, *105*
Cambrensis, Giraldus, 23

Campion, Thomas, 62
Candying, of herbs and flowers, 63
Carmontelle, 130, 156
Carpenter's work, 41; and outdoor rooms, 42–43; *43, 60*
Carpet bedding, 120; and affinities with embroidery, 120–21; and William Morris, 125
Carpets, English, 76; as grass analogues, 115
Carpets, Persian, 67–68, 71–76; as spirit of the garden, 68, 71–73, *75;* as practical floor coverings, 73; and flowers, 74, *75;* and hunting and animals, 74
Castles: as dwellings, 21; decoration of, 23–26; obsolescence of, 38
Cathay, legend of, 83–85
Cave paintings, Paleolithic, 1
Chardin, Sir John, 71
Charles VIII, and Naples, 37
Chaucer, Geoffrey, 20–21, 39, 61
*Cherry Ripe, 110*
Cheyne, George, 55
Chinoiserie, 86–89; disenchantment with, 89–91, 100
Chintz: origins of, 79; as decoration, 81–83; imitations of, 83
Chosroes I, 73
Christianity, 16–17
Churchill, Sir Winston, 79
Cities, attitudes to, 97, 122–24, 169
Clark, J.T.C., 119
Clark, Kenneth, xiii
Climatotherapy, 156–57
Cloister gardens. *See* Gardens, monastic
Clothing, embroidered, 54, 61
Cloths, painted and stained: medieval, 25–26; Elizabethan, 49; Indian, 77–79, *78, 80*
Colonna, Francesco, 49
*Connoisseur,* 97
Conservatories, 148–49; domestic, 150–52, 155–59, *158;* American, 150, 152; and exotic plants, 152; and health, 156–57; resurgence of, 177. *See also* Winter gardens
Constable, John, 131
Cook, Clarence, 145
*Cottages ornés,* 99, 154
Country life: and Romans, 3; and medieval courtiers, 33; 18th-century attitudes to, 97–100, 104, 108, *110, 112;* and godliness, 98; Victorian nostalgia for, 122–25; and modern sensibility, 169

Cowper, William, 122, 150
*Craftsman,* 165, 172, 175
Crescentiis, 21
Crete, and decorative art, 1–2
Crystal Palace, 119, 167
Cyzicene, 6, 170

Daniell, Thomas, 91
Daniell, William, 91
da Vinci, Leonardo, 74
*Decameron,* 21
de Jandun, Jean, 23
Delany, Mary, 99, 102, 109, 111
de Serres, Olivier, 40
Devonshire tapestries, 31–32
de Warville, Brissot, 132
Dickens, Charles, 123
d'Orleans, Charles, 33
Downing, Andrew Jackson: and landscape and culture, 106; and environmentalism, 128; and window blinds, 131
Drakelowe Hall, *114,* 115
Dufour, Joseph, 135, 139, 143

Edison, Thomas, 169
*Eldorado, 138*
Elizabeth I, 48, 76
Embroidery: Tudor, xiii, *40, 42, 43,* 49–66; as secular pursuit, 50; as accomplishment, 50; status of, 50; affinities with knot gardening, 59–66, *60;* and Chinese style, 88; and 18th-century landscape, 101–11, *102, 103, 104, 105, 109;* American, 104–8, *107;* and 19th century gardens, 119–20
Embroidery motifs, sources of: garden and hedgerow, 52–53; plant symbolism, 52–55; herbals and botanical works, 55–56; exotic plants, 57–59
*Emma,* 95
Environmentalism, 106, 127, 128
Erasmus, 48
Ettinghausen, Richard, 68, 73
Europamudigkeit, 87
Evans, Joan, 1, 25
Evelyn, John: and embroidery, 50; and gardens, 52; and chintz, 82; and chinoiserie, 87, 88, 89; and garden scenes, 100

"Factory papers," 85
Fairchild, Thomas, 100
Fastolf, Sir John, 28

# Index

185

Fences, American attitudes to, 118, 175
*Fête Dieu*, 36
*Fêtes champêtres*, 99, 111, 156
*Fêtes galantes*, 111
Fiennes, Celia, 94, 101
Fireplaces, 39; decoration of, 46, 113
"Fishing Lady" embroidery, *107*
Fishponds, 65
Floors, 23, 48, 73, 74
Flower gardening: and women, 52–53, 111, 119; and virtue, 53, 119; and contentment, 119
Flowers: and Greeks, 2; and Romans, 17; and symbolism, 16–17, 53, 55; and monastic gardens 18; and decoration of abbeys and churches, 18–20; and castle gardens, 20; and orchards, 21; and decoration of castles and manor houses, 23–24; in French Parliament, 24; in Tudor gardens, 40–41; in Tudor houses, 45, 47; and Londoners, 46, 100; and Shakespeare, 46; and use in medicines and perfumes, 47; increasing interest in, 56; and Versailles, 66; declining popularity of, 65–66; return to gardens, 117–19
Flowers, exotic: influence on gardening and garden design, 46, 57, 118; sources of, 118; and greenhouse culture, 118, 121, 152; and William Morris, 125
Flowers, paintings of: in medieval castles and houses, 24–25; in Tudor houses, 45
Focillon, 26
Foot, Paul, 130
Forcing houses. *See* Greenhouses
Fortunatus, Venantius, 16, 18
*Franklin Hanging, 40*
French windows, 152, 170
Frescoes: Cretan, 2; Christian, 16; at Avignon, 30, 33. *See also* Wallpaintings
Friar Odoric of Pordenone, 84
Froissart, 23
Fuchs, Leonhart, 56
Fuller, Thomas, 58, 67

Gad's Hill, 123
Gainsborough, Thomas, 103, 108
Gardening: and awareness of nature, 28; and affinities with embroidery, 59–66, 119–20, 121
Garden paintings, Roman, 8–13, *11, 12*
Gardens: Greek, 2–3; Roman, 3–4; monastic, 17–20; church and cathedral, 20;

castle, 20–21, 23; medieval 20–23, *22;* Italian, 37–38; Tudor, 39–46, *40, 42, 43;* in Tudor towns, 45; French style, 65–66; Persian, 68–71, *69, 70;* minature, 71; 18th-century, 93–96; 19th-century, 117–22; suburban, 175, *176*
Garden scenes, trompe l'oeil, 100
Gardens, flower and pleasure: ascendancy of, 40–41; as female domains, 52
Gardens, herb and vegetable, and women, 21, 52–53
Gardner, Eugene C., 154
Gaskell, Mrs., 121
Gautier, Theophile, 137
*Georgics*, 3, 18, 104
Gerard, John: and naturalistic decoration, 48; and strewing, 48; and women and gardens, 52; and flowers, 53; and embroidery, 55; and tulips, 58; and gardening and embroidery, 61
Gilpin, William, 115
Girtin, Thomas, 131
Glasier, Bruce, 128
Glass: substitutes for, 4, 39; scarcity of, 39; improvements in quality of 151; and size of glass sheets, 151; and tax, 151
Goldsmith, Margaret, 172
Googe, Barnaby, 45
Gorhambury, 65
Gosse, Edmund, 63
Greenhouses: Roman, 4; and exotic plants, 121; as forcing houses, 148, 157; ideal form of, 157
Grose, Francis, 38
Grottoes, and embroidery, 64
Ground embroidery, 65

Habitat, ideal, 6
Hadrian: and Prima Porta, xii; and Vale of Tempe, 6, 96
*Haha, 95*
Hakluyt, Richard, 58
Hancock, Thomas, 89, 106–7
Hanmer, Sir Thomas, 66, 96
Hardwick Hall, 31, 39
Harrison, William: and Tudor gardens, 40; and wall hangings, 49; and exotic plants, 57
Hastings, Lady, 26
Hatfield House, 65
Hawe, Stephen, 42
Hazlitt, William, 123

Heating systems: limitations of, 147; improvements in, 151, 169
Henderson, Peter, 119
Herbals, 55–56
Herbert, Sir Thomas, 71
Herculaneum, and wall paintings, 7, 10
Herrad of Landsperg, 18
Hilliard, Nicholas, 54
Holbein, Hans, 76
Holinshead, 50
Holland, Lady, 100
Holland, Philomen, 7
Homer, 2
Honour, Hugh: and tastes in decoration, 80; and Cathay, 83
Houses: embroidered pictures of, 102, 103, 106; as symbols of order and security, *104*, 106; underground, 170
Houses, design of: Roman, 4, 5; medieval, 23, 27; Renaissance Italian, 37–38; Tudor, 38–39, 51; neoclassical, 100; picturesque, 152–55, *153*
Houses, interiors of: medieval, 21, 23; Tudor, 39, 51; neoclassical, 100, 113; Victorian, 120, 152, 159; American, 154–55, 161; modern, 169–70, *171*
Houses, relationship with surroundings: Roman, 13; Renaissance, 38–39, 41; 19th-century, 152; American, 152–54, 170–72
Humphrey, Zephine, 165
Hunting: appeal of, 28–30, 32; and awareness of nature, 29; and influence on decorative art, 30–32; and Persia, 74; and embroidery, 108–12
*Hunting the Deer, 31*

*Iliad, 2*
*Illustrated London News*, 143
Illustrations, botanical, as models for embroiderers, 55–59
Illustrators, botanical, 58–59
*Impluvium, 4*
Insects, symbolism of, 55
"Interiorscaping," 177
International Style, 168–69
Irwin, John, 79

Jackson, John, 88, 131
Jackson, John Baptist, 91, 113, 114
James, Henry, 154
*Jardin anglais*, 111
Jardin des Plantes, Paris, 59, 119

Jardin d'Hiver, Lyon, *151*
Johnson, Samuel, 66, 108
Johnson, Thomas, 56
Jonchée, custom of, 23

Kelmscott, 127, 128, *129*
Kent, William, 101
Kerr, Robert, 156
Kew, 111, 118, 149, 150
King, Donald, 31
Knight, Richard Payne, 117
Knossos, and frescoes, 2
Knot gardens, 41–42; and embroidery, 60, 61, 62; and bedding out, 118, 119
Knowle cottage, *153*

Labors of the months, and decorative motifs, 33
*Ladies Companion to the Flower Garden*, 119
*Ladies Magazine of Gardening*, 117, 119
Landscape, attitudes to, xiv; Greek, 2; Roman, 3, 6, 7, 10, 13, 97; medieval, 15–16, 20, 23; neoclassical, 93–94, 95–96; American, 106, 118, 141–43
Landscape gardening: in France, 93–94; in England, 94–96
Langford, T., 148
Lawns: medieval, 21; 18th-century, 96; significance of, in England and U. S., 106; as *tapis verts*, 115; containment of, 117; popularity in U.S., 118, 121; difficulties of maintaining, 121; likeness to velvet, 121; mowing machines, 121; and American suburbs, 122, 175
Lawson, William, 41, 46
"Leaf embroidery," and Berlin woolwork, 121
Le Breton, Guillaume, 26
Le Brun, Cornelius, 71
Le Corbusier, 169, 176
Leland, John, 38
Lemnius, Levimus, 47
Le Notre, Andre, 66, 94
Lighting, interior: in Roman houses, 7; in Tudor houses, 51; limitations of, 147; improvements in, 151; in modern houses, 169–70
Lipman, Jean, 143
*Little Dorritt*, 123
Livia, Empress, 8
Loggias, 165
London: and window boxes, 45; and nursery trade, 45, 57; and area and population, 97;

# Index

187

and weekend villas, 97; and flowers, 101;
and panoramas, 131
London, Tower of, 25
Long galleries, 39, 147
Loos, Adolf, 168
Lorraine, Claude, 94–95
Lotto, Lorenzo, 74
Loudon, John Claudius: and botany and
embroidery, 111; and winter gardens, 149,
155; and verandas, 152; and conserva-
tories, 156
Loudon, Mrs. John Claudius: and gardening
and embroidery, 119–20; and carpet bed-
ding, 121

McClelland, Nancy, 133
Maeterlinck, Maurice, 46, 57, 58
Mandeville, Sir John, 84
Markham, Gervase, 40, 62
Marlowe, Christopher, 62
Marshall, Adam Davie, 24
Martial, 3
Martineau, Harriet, 133–34
Mary, Queen of Scotland, 50
Maumene, 20
Maupassant, Guy de, 156
Mesdag, Hendrik, 131
Millefleurs, 35–36
Mollet, Andre, 65
Montague, Lord, 47
*Monuments of Paris, 137*
Morland, George, 108–9
Morris, William: and walls, xv, *126;* and
gardening and embroidery, 62; and
medievalism, 124–27; and aims, 127; and
town planning, 127; and trees, 127; and
environmentalism, 128, and naturalism,
128–29; and simplicity in decoration, 129,
169; and conservatories, 156; and Arts and
Crafts Movement, 163; and windows, 176
Moryson, Fynes, 41
Mounts, 42
Muffet, Thomas, 55

Nash, John, 155
Nashe, Thomas, 46
Needlepainting, 108–9
Needler, Henry, 98
*Noble Pastoral, The, 35*
Norbury Park, 115
Nurseries, plant: and Rome, 4, and London,
45, 57

*Odyssey,* and landscape, 2
Orangeries, *102,* 148
Orchards: appeal of, 20–21, 46; and Tudor
towns, 45
Ornamental farms, 99
*Oscillum,* 10

Palladianism, 100
Panoramas, landscape, 130–31
*Paradeisoi,* 13
Paradise gardens, 17–18, 20
*Paradisi in sole Paradisus Terrestris,* 40, 43,
55, 57
Paris, Matthew, 67
Parker, Henry, 88
Parker, Rozsika, 103, 104
Parkinson, John: and vegetable gardens, 40;
and tree arbors, 43; and strewing, 47, 48;
and embroidery, 55; and exotic plants, 57,
58; and gardening and embroidery, 62;
and plant experiments, 63; and orange
trees, 148
Parterres, 65
Paxton, Joseph, 120
Pearsall, Derek, 17, 32
*Peasants Hunting Rabbits with Ferrets, 30*
Peixotto, Ernest, 172
Pepys, Samuel: and French style, 65; and
aversion to flowers, 66; and chintz, 82
Pergolas, 175
Peristyles, Roman, 4; and garden paintings,
10–12, *11*
Pero de Nino, 32
Phebus, Gaston, 29
Pictures, embroidered, 108
Plants, symbolism of, 53–55
"Plantscaping," 177
Platt, Sir Hugh, 45, 63
Platter, Sir Thomas, 61
Pleasances. *See* Orchards
Pliny, the elder, 3, 9
Pliny, the younger, 4–6
Poggio Reale, villa of, 37, 38
Pole screens, 102
Polloxfen, 81
Polo, Marco, 83–84
Pompeii: wall paintings, 7–9; tomb
paintings, 9; houses and gardens, 10–12;
garden paintings, 10–12
Pope, Alexander, 67, 96
Porches, 154, 157; as architectural hyphens,
175

Porter, Rufus, 141–43, *142*
Potemkin, Prince, 148
Poussin, Nicolas, 94
Price, Uvedale, 99
Prima Porta, villa of: and comfort, xiii; and
  paintings, 7–8, *8*
Puckler-Muskau, Prince, 119
Pugin, Augustus, 134

Ray, John, 97
Rea, John, 66
Red House, 125, 127
Repton, Humphry: and landscape gardens,
  117; and shrubberies, 118; and house
  design, 155; and conservatories, 156
Roe, Sir Thomas, 79
Rohde, Eleanour, 42, 46
Romanticism, 94
Roof gardens, Roman, 3
Rosa, Salvator, 94
Rousseau, Jean-Jacques, 98
Royal Botanic Society, 149
Rugs. *See* Carpets
Rushes, as matting, 68
Ruskin, John, 163

St. Augustine, 17
St. Radegund, 18
Sallust, 7
Salter, Elizabeth, 17
Samplers, 107–9
Sanborn, Kate, 134
Sandby, Paul, *114*
*Savages of the Pacific Ocean*, 136
Saxton, Christopher, 98
Scenic wallpapers, 130–40; popularity of,
  132–34; geographical range, 134–36;
  subjects, 135, *136, 137, 138*; didactic
  function of, 137–39; American, 139;
  demise of, 144–45
*Scientific American*, 141, *142*
Scott, Frank J.: and lawns, 121; and founda-
  tion planting, 152; and suburbs, 175
Sedding, John, 122
Selmiston, Thomas, 50
Serlio, Sebastiano, 38
Seward, Anna, 115–16
Shaftesbury, Lord, 94
Shah Abbas I, 73, 76
Shakespeare, William: and spring, xiv, 46;
  and winter, xiv, 46; and knot gardens, 41;

and flowers, 46; and gardening and
  embroidery, 61
Shebbeare, John, 91
*Sheepshearing, 33*
Sheldon, Ralph, 98
Sherrington, Grace, 53
Sherwin, Will, 83
Shorleyker, Richard, 56
Sidonious, Appollinarus, 15
Sleeping porches, 154
Smollett, Tobias, 98
*Spectator*, 95
Spenser, Edmund, 62
Stalker, John, 88
Steele, Richard, 96
Stent, Peter, 56
Stevenson, J. J., 157
Stoke, Edith, embroidered hangings at, 101,
  *102, 103*
Storch, Chevalier, 148
Stow, John, 45, 46
Stowe, Harriet Beecher, 159, 162–63
Strabo, and Campanian plain, 6
Strabo, Walafrid, 18
Strewing: of floors and mantles, xiv; of
  churches, 18; of castles and manor houses,
  23–24; in Tudor houses, 47–48; in France,
  48; harards of, 48; substitutes for, 68
Stubbes, Philip, 61
Stumpwork, and outlandish plants, 63–64,
  *64*
Sullivan, Louis, 168
Summer houses, Tudor, 44; suburban, 97; as
  outdoor rooms, 147; replacements for, 148
*Sunset* magazine, 172
Surfleet, Richard, 41
Swayze, Jay, 170
Switzer, Richard, 96

Tapestries: origins of, 25; medieval, 25–36;
  manufacture of, 26–27; as substitutes for
  wall paintings, 27; as northern decorations, 27–28; portability of, 27; as street
  decorations, 28; as ideal wall coverings,
  36; and the Chinese style, 88; and 18th-
  century houses, 111–13; adulteration and
  decline of, 112–13; and William Morris,
  125–27
Tapestry maps, 98
Tapestry subjects: the chase, 28–32, *30, 31,*
  111–12; country labors, 32, 33, *33, 34,*

# Index

111–12; verdures, or wilderness scenes, 32–36; "millefleurs," 35–36, *35*
*Tapis verts*, 115
Tavernier, Jean Baptiste, 79, 81
Taylor, John, 59, 82
Teniers, David, 111, *112*
Terminology, shared by gardening and embroidery, 62, 63
Terry, Edward, 79
*Theatrum Botanicum*, 48
Thomas, Keith, 53
Thornton, Robert, 111
*Toiles de Bruges*, 26
*Toiles peintes*, 26
Tomb paintings, Roman, 9
Toronto, Winter Garden Theatre, *164*, 165
Toronto Horticultural Society, 150
Townsend, George Alfred, 133
Tree arbors, 42–44
Tree houses, *19*, 44, *44*, 69, 147
Trees, artificial, 71, 163
Trees, paintings of, 25, 48–49, 115
*Tres Riches Heures*, 32–33
Trevelyan, Thomas, 61
*Triclinia*, 4, *5*, 6, 147
Tulips, rage for, 58
Tusser, Thomas, 52, 55

Valances, embroidered, 42–43, *43*, 51
Vallet, Pierre, 59
Van der Rohe, Mies, 168
*Velum*, 6
Verandas, 99, 152, 175
Verdures. *See* Tapestry subjects
Versailles, Palace of, 66, 94
Virgil, and rural life, 3, 18, 104
Vitruvius, and wall painting, 7, 9
Von Humboldt, Alexander, 136
*Voyages of Captain Cook*, *136*

*Wagner Garden Carpet*, 72
Wainscoting, 24, 125
Wall painting, techniques of: Roman, 7; medieval, 24; American, 140–41
Wall paintings: Greek, 2; Roman, xiii, 7–13, *10*; at Prima Porta, 7–8, *8*; in Roman gardens, 8–13, *11*, *12*; medieval, 24–25; Tudor, 48–49; at Kew, 99; 18th-century, *114*, 115–16; Victorian, 123; American, 140–45, *142*; Nova Scotian, 143, *144*; in underground houses, 170

Wallpaper: Chinese landscape or export papers, 85–86, *86*, *87*; as substitute for tapestries, 88, 113; and Chinese style, 88–89, *90*; and William Morris, 128; machine production of, 143. *See also* Scenic wallpapers
Walpole, Horace: and landscaping, 95; and ornamental farms, 99; and tapestry, 113
Ward, Dr. Nathaniel Bagshaw, 118, 159
Ward, Stephen, 159, 161
Wardian cases, 157, 159–63, *161*, *162*, *163*
Ware, Isaac, 91
Warner, Richard, 91
Watteau, Jean-Antoine, 111
Webb, Sydney and Beatrice, 93
Whately, Thomas, 99
Wheatley, Francis, 108, 110
Wilcox, Thomas, 55
Wilderness tapestries. *See* Tapestry subjects
Williams, Raymond, 102–3, 123
Wilton, countess of, 120
Window blinds, translucent, 131
Window boxes: Roman, 4; Tudor, 45
Windows: and Roman houses, 4, 7; "Cyzicene," 6, 147; and castles and manor houses, 21, 27; and Tudor houses, 39; and long galleries, 39; as movable chattels, 39; improvements to, 113; limitations of, 147; and glass tax, 151; size of, 151, 154; and French, 152; placement of, 154, 170; as glass walls, 147, 169–70, 176; and views, 170
Winter, dread of, xiv, 18, 45, 46
Winter gardens, 147–50, 152; as public spaces, 149–50, *151*; plant arrangements in, 150; decline of, 165; and technology of, 167
Wolsey, Cardinal, 48, 76
Wooburn Farm, 99
*Woodcutters, The*, *34*
*Woodpecker, The*, *126*
Woolf, Virginia, 120, 159
Wootten, Sir Henry, 94
Wootton, John, 108, *109*, 111–12
Worlidge, John, 45, 62, 66
Wright, Frank Lloyd, 170–73

Xenophon: and hunting parks, 13; and Persian gardens, 68; and Persian carpets, 73

Yale, Elihu, 88
Young, Arthur, 108
*Young Man amongst the Roses*, 54

*Zimmerlaube*, 159
Zola, Emile, 157
Zuber, Jean, 135–36, 140, 143

*Interior Landscapes* by Ronald Rees
Designed by Glen Burris
Set in Aster text and Cochin display by Brushwood Graphics, Inc.
Printed on 70-lb. Patina Matte by The Maple Press Company